Tarawa, Roi-Namur, and Eniwetok, 1943–44

Japanese Infantryman

VERSUS

US Marine Rifleman

Gregg Adams

T0322912

Illustrated by Johnny Shumate

OSPREY PUBLISHING
Bloomsbury Publishing Plc
Kemp House, Chawley Park, Cumnor Hill, Oxford OX2 9PH, UK
29 Earlsfort Terrace, Dublin 2, Ireland
1385 Broadway, 5th Floor, New York, NY 10018, USA
E-mail: info@ospreypublishing.com
www.ospreypublishing.com

OSPREY is a trademark of Osprey Publishing Ltd

First published in Great Britain in 2023

A catalog record for this book is available from the British Library.

ISBN: PB 9781472857910; eBook 9781472857897;
ePDF 9781472857927; XML 9781472857903

23 24 25 26 27   10 9 8 7 6 5 4 3 2 1

Maps by www.bounford.com
Index by Rob Munro
Typeset by PDQ Digital Media Solutions, Bungay, UK
Printed and bound in India by Replika Press Private Ltd.

Osprey Publishing supports the Woodland Trust, the UK's leading
woodland conservation charity.

To find out more about our authors and books visit
www.ospreypublishing.com. Here you will find extracts, author
interviews, details of forthcoming events and the option to sign up for
our newsletter.

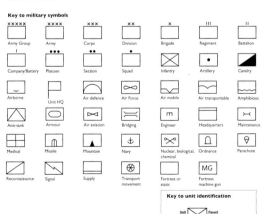

Acknowledgments

Research for this book was aided by the US Marine Corps' History
Division, US Navy History and Heritage Command, US Army
Combined Arms Research Library, and the US Army Center for Military
History, which have digitally scanned thousands of historic original
documents and photographs and have made these available to the public
via the internet. The author also thanks Mark Stille for providing copies
of relevant volumes from the postwar Japanese Monographs series.

CONTENTS

Introduction

At 0832hrs, November 20, 1943, Landing Vehicles Tracked (LVTs) carrying the 2d Marines crossed their line of departure offshore of Betio Island, Tarawa Atoll in the Gilbert Islands. They reached the beach 45 minutes later and 76 hours of intense combat began that resulted in the capture of Betio. This assault was a brutal combat test of US amphibious warfare doctrine, organization, tactics, and capabilities. Tarawa Atoll's capture was followed in February 1944 by the rapid US seizure of the Japanese-held Kwajalein Atoll and Eniwetok Atoll in the Marshall Islands.

The Gilberts and Marshalls are part of Micronesia, a large region of the Pacific Ocean that also includes the Caroline, Mariana, and Palau islands. While the latter three groups include volcanic islands (e.g. Guam), the Gilberts and Marshalls are chains of coral atolls. An atoll is a ring-shaped coral reef encircling a lagoon. Atolls' highest elevations range from just a few feet to

A US Marine throws a grenade during the fight for Betio Island, November 20–23, 1943. Note the sand hill at far right, possibly a Japanese defensive position, and the fixed bayonet on the M1 rifle at right. (USMC 63658, courtesy Naval History and Heritage Command)

tens of feet above sea level. The land area of an atoll is small while the lagoon may be large; Kwajalein Atoll's lagoon, for example, is 839 square miles while its 97 islands and islets encompass only 6.3 square miles of land.

The United States' acquisition of the Philippine islands after the Spanish–American War (1898) made the US military responsible for defending them. The growth of Imperial Japan's military forces, boosted by their victory in the Russo-Japanese War (1904–05), led US planners to view Japan as the major threat to the Philippines. With the bulk of the US Navy's assets located in home waters, a fleet would have to traverse the Pacific to defend the Philippines and establish naval control of the Western Pacific. This fleet required anchorages and facilities across the Pacific to enable refueling, resupplying, maintenance, and light repairs.

Following World War I, Japan received control of Central Pacific islands that had been ruled by Imperial Germany. Japan could use these islands as bases to interdict the Central Pacific route that US forces would have to sail to reach the Philippines. Knowing that advanced fleet bases would be needed, and desiring to deny similar bases to their enemy, the US Navy and US Marine Corps began studying how to seize and defend islands located in the Central Pacific. Concepts were developed and incorporated in the joint Army–Navy plan for war against the Japanese Empire. This plan was known as War Plan Orange.

Before 1940, US military planners thought the Japanese had heavily fortified their Micronesian possessions. In fact, although access to Micronesia was tightly controlled by the Japanese, their fortification of the islands did not begin until 1940. In January 1941, the Imperial Japanese Navy (IJN) activated the 6th Base Force and 6th Defense Unit at Kwajalein Atoll. The emphasis was originally on building airbases, fleet anchorages, and forward submarine bases. Defenses were designed to deter and defeat small-scale raids. IJN ground forces on Kwajalein on December 7 consisted of 204 officers and men of the 6th Defense Unit, which had received 24 twin-mounted 127mm Type 89 dual-purpose guns, intended to engage air or surface targets, in October 1941. By December, most of the IJN personnel based in Micronesia were construction, administration, supply, or aviation personnel.

Japanese defenses in the Marshalls, and the occupied Gilberts, remained weak until late 1942. Only after the August 1942 raid by US Marines on Makin Atoll in the Gilberts did the Japanese start to fortify islands in both groups seriously. Tarawa Atoll was occupied by IJN Special Naval Landing Forces (SNLF) troops

MAP KEY

Operations in the Gilbert and Marshall islands, 1942–44

1   September 15, 1942: The 6th Yokosuka SNLF occupies and begins to fortify Tarawa Atoll and Makin Atoll in the Gilbert Islands.

2   February 1943: The 6th Yokosuka SNLF is reinforced and redesignated the 3d Special Base Force (SBF).

3   November 20–23, 1943: The 2d Marine Division captures Tarawa Atoll.

4   November 20–24, 1943: Elements of the US Army's 27th Division capture Makin Atoll.

5   November 21–26, 1943: The V Amphibious Corps (VAC) Reconnaissance Company secures Apamama Atoll.

6   January 4, 1944: The IJA's 1st Amphibious Brigade (less detachments) lands on Eniwetok Atoll and starts building fortifications.

7   January 31, 1944: US forces seize Majuro Atoll.

8   January 31–February 4, 1944: The 4th Marine Division and the US Army's 7th Infantry Division capture Kwajalein Atoll.

9   February 18–22, 1944: The VAC's Tactical Group (TacGrp) 1 captures Eniwetok Atoll.

10   March 4, 1944: The 4th Marine Air Wing, based on Roi Island (Kwajalein Atoll) and Majuro Atoll, starts a bombing campaign against the bypassed Japanese-held atolls of Wotje, Maloelap, Mille, and Jaluit to keep these neutralized.

Major Earl H. "Pete" Ellis provided the intellectual foundation for America's amphibious campaign against Imperial Japan in World War II when he developed Operations Plan 712, *Advanced Base Operations in Micronesia*, in 1921. Ellis died on May 12, 1923, on the Japanese-held island of Koror in the Caroline Islands. Despite rumors claiming the Japanese killed him, the US Marine Corps states the likely cause of death was alcohol poisoning and nephritis. Ellis Hall, the home of the US Marine Corps' Command and Staff College at Quantico, Virginia, is named in his honor. (US Marine Corps)

and became their main center of defense in the Gilberts. In the Marshalls, the Japanese built up strong defenses on the eastern atolls of Wotje, Maloelap, Mille, and Jaluit using both IJN ground troops and Imperial Japanese Army (IJA) units. This buildup stemmed from the Japanese assumption that these locations, along with Tarawa Atoll, would be the first US attack objectives. Kwajalein Atoll, in the center of the Marshalls, remained lightly defended. Eniwetok Atoll, in the western Marshalls, was essentially undefended until January 1944.

The expected major naval campaign in the Central Pacific did not occur with the start of the Pacific War. US losses at Pearl Harbor on December 7, 1941, Allied defeats in the Pacific (including the loss of the Philippines in February 1942), the IJN's defeat at the battle of Midway in June 1942, and the US counteroffensive at Guadalcanal in the Solomon Islands starting in August 1942, shifted major operations to the South Pacific and New Guinea. From July 1942 until the fall of 1943, fighting in the Pacific was conducted mainly in and around the Solomons and New Guinea.

New ships were added to the US Navy's Pacific Fleet during 1943 and new air and ground units were prepared for combat. By October 1943 the Pacific Fleet had six fleet carriers, six light fleet carriers, six new fast battleships, and seven modernized prewar battleships. These were supported by a large number of cruisers, destroyers, escort carriers, amphibious vessels, and auxiliaries. This fleet, now larger than the IJN's Combined Fleet, was ready to advance. The first target was Tarawa Atoll in the Gilberts. Tarawa Atoll is located 540 miles south-southeast of Kwajalein Atoll, 1,005 miles northeast of Guadalcanal, 695 miles northwest of Funafuti (the closest American airbase), and 2,390 miles southwest of Pearl Harbor in the Hawaiian Islands. It was Japan's farthest eastern defense bastion in the Pacific. Its capture would provide an airbase for US land-based aircraft to strike the Marshalls. Once Tarawa was secured, the Marshalls would be invaded. The Central Pacific drive of War Plan Orange was now underway.

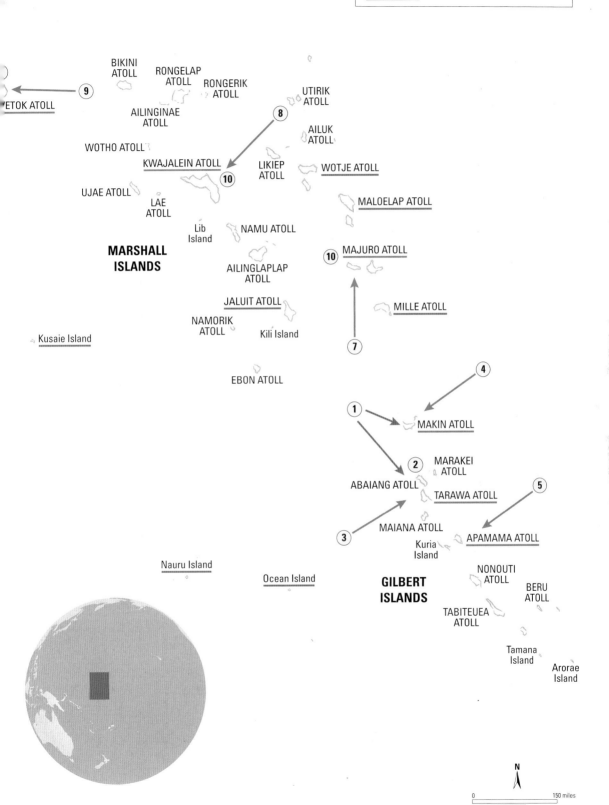

MAKIN ATOLL — Captured by US forces by February 25, 1944
MILLE ATOLL — Held by Japanese forces until war's end

BIKINI ATOLL
RONGELAP ATOLL
RONGERIK ATOLL
UTIRIK ATOLL
AILINGINAE ATOLL
AILUK ATOLL
WOTHO ATOLL
KWAJALEIN ATOLL
LIKIEP ATOLL
WOTJE ATOLL
ETOK ATOLL
UJAE ATOLL
MALOELAP ATOLL
LAE ATOLL
Lib Island
NAMU ATOLL

MARSHALL ISLANDS

MAJURO ATOLL
AILINGLAPLAP ATOLL
MILLE ATOLL
JALUIT ATOLL
NAMORIK ATOLL
Kili Island
Kusaie Island
EBON ATOLL

MAKIN ATOLL

MARAKEI ATOLL
ABAIANG ATOLL
TARAWA ATOLL
MAIANA ATOLL
APAMAMA ATOLL
Kuria Island

Nauru Island
Ocean Island

GILBERT ISLANDS

NONOUTI ATOLL
BERU ATOLL
TABITEUEA ATOLL
Tamana Island
Arorae Island

N

0   150 miles
0   150km

The Opposing Sides

The US invasions of the Gilberts and Marshalls pitted US Marines against a range of Japanese ground defenders, both IJN and IJA. On Tarawa Atoll, the veteran 2d Marine Division fought IJN troops of the 3d SBF (formed from the 6th Yokosuka SNLF), 7th Sasebo SNLF, and 111th Construction Unit. On the twin islands of Roi-Namur (Kwajalein Atoll in the Marshalls), the new 4th Marine Division encountered a battalion-sized detachment of the 61st Naval Guard Unit and an ad hoc force of IJN construction, supply, and aviation personnel. On Eniwetok Atoll, the separate 22d Marines engaged the main body of the IJA's 1st Amphibious Brigade and a small detachment of the 61st Naval Guard Unit.

This study concentrates on US Marine Corps units and their IJN and IJA ground opponents that fought on atolls and islands of the Gilberts and Marshalls. Greater detail is provided on IJN ground troops – SNLFs, Special Base Forces (SBFs), Guard Units, and improvised infantry – but this section begins with a discussion of US amphibious doctrine and its prewar development followed by highlights of Japanese island-defense doctrine as it was during these operations.

This is a modern-day image of Wake Atoll. In December 1941 Wake was held by the US Marine Corps' 1st Defense Battalion. On December 11, a Japanese assault was repulsed by coastal artillery and aircraft before troops could be landed. On December 23, Wake was captured by the 2d Maizuru SNLF. This view shows the narrow land areas around the lagoon and how installations, such as an airfield, could occupy a significant portion of land. (US Air Force)

DOCTRINE AND TACTICS

US amphibious warfare doctrine

Major Earl H. "Pete" Ellis USMC began his *Advanced Base Operations in Micronesia* study with these words:

> In order to impose our will upon Japan, it will be necessary for us to project our fleet and land forces across the Pacific and wage war in Japanese waters. To effect this requires that we have sufficient bases to support the fleet, both during its projection and afterwards. As the matter stands at present, we cannot count upon the use of any bases west of Hawaii except those which we may seize from the enemy after the opening of hostilities. Moreover, the continued occupation of the Marshall, Caroline, and Pelew [Paulau] Islands by the Japanese (now holding them under mandate of the League of Nations) invests them with a series of emergency bases flanking any line of communications across the Pacific throughout a distance of 2300 miles. The reduction and occupation of these islands and the establishment of the necessary bases therein, as a preliminary phase of the hostilities, is practically imperative. (Ellis 1921: 29)

In his study, Ellis assessed possible atolls and islands to be seized. He estimated likely enemy defenses and US landing forces for different objectives. He also identified key factors for successful ship-to-shore assaults including disembarkation of troops from transports into landing boats, organization and control of landing boats as they advanced toward the beach, composition and equipment of combat teams to conduct assaults, and the roles of air and naval-gunfire support, intelligence, and communications.

Ellis's study became the foundation upon which the US Marine Corps began to develop amphibious-warfare doctrine. In November 1933, the US Marine Corps Schools at Quantico, Virginia, suspended classes and put all hands to work writing a detailed doctrine for amphibious operations. The resulting document, *Tentative Manual for Landing Operations*, was issued January 1934. In 1935 an updated version was issued by the US Navy under the title *Tentative Landing Operations Manual.* Another revision was issued in 1938 as Fleet Training Publication 167 (FTP-167) *Landing Operations Doctrine*, which became US amphibious-warfare doctrine throughout World War II. A modified version of FTP-167 was issued by the US Army as FM 31-5 *Landing Operations on Hostile Shores.*

FTP-167 covered amphibious warfare in depth. Chapters examined planning, organization, command and control, ship-to-shore movement, naval-gunfire support, aviation support, communications, field artillery, tanks, chemicals, smoke, and logistics. Example charts and tables provided

BELOW LEFT
USS *Belle Grove* (LSD-2) at sea. Entering service in the summer of 1943, the Landing Ship Dock (LSD) was a significant innovation in amphibious transports. LSDs featured a floodable well deck. Loaded landing craft were floated into the well and then the water pumped out. The well deck was again flooded when LSDs arrived at assault areas and the landing craft made their way toward shore under their own power. LSDs were crucial for providing the ability to deliver M4 medium tanks preloaded in Landing Craft Mechanized (LCMs) to beaches within minutes of the arrival of the first assault waves. (NH107618, courtesy of the Naval History and Heritage Command)

BELOW RIGHT
USS *Callaway* (APA-35). The "Auxiliary Personnel Attack" was an ocean-going troop transport specially configured to carry its own assault landing craft, usually Landing Craft, Vehicle and Personnel (LCVPs). Usually, one Battalion Landing Team (BLT) was assigned to an APA. When necessary, assault troops would transfer from their APA to LSTs in order to load in LVTs. APAs were built to allow rapid unloading of men and equipment into landing craft so that transports could, if necessary, leave the area off a beachhead if the enemy tried to attack the amphibious force. (US Navy)

This rifleman of BLT 1/6 is advancing toward Japanese positions on Betio Island as part of the 2d Marine Division's attack on D+2. BLT 1/6 came ashore on the western end of Betio on D+1 at 1800hrs following the clearing of that part of the island.

Weapons, dress, and equipment

This Marine is armed with a .30-caliber M1 Garand semiautomatic rifle (**1**) with an M1905 bayonet fixed (**2**).

He is wearing a 1941-type utility uniform with camouflage pattern. This was a two-piece suit made of heavy, sage-green, herringbone twill cotton. The jacket (**3**) had three flapless pockets, one on the left chest and two on the front hips. It was secured by four metal, riveted buttons embossed with "U.S. Marine Corps," though the top button near the collar was rarely fastened. The trousers (**4**) had a button fly and four pockets. There were several arrangements of pockets on the trousers, depending upon manufacturer. He wears leggings (**5**) and brown service shoes (**6**). His helmet (**7**) is the M1 model with a camouflage helmet cover.

Marines dropped their packs and any other equipment that they considered unnecessary in the tropical heat in order to fight. As well as his canteen (**8**) and bayonet scabbard (**9**), this Marine wears an M1 Garand M1923 cartridge belt (**10**) with ten M1 cartridge pockets and a six-pocket cotton bandoleer (**11**) across his left shoulder. He also carries one M1924 first-aid pouch (**12**).

templates for timing waves of landing craft, allocating troop and equipment space on landing craft, loading landing craft from transports, and naval-gunfire support. One of FTP-167's strengths was that it articulated the rationale behind the doctrine for ship-to-shore assault movement and naval-gunfire support. The manual explained that in an amphibious assault, ship-to-shore movement was an integral part of an infantry attack: "A landing operation against opposition is, in effect, an assault on an organized or unorganized defensive position modified by substituting initially ships' gunfire for that of light, medium, and heavy field artillery, and frequently, carrier-based aviation for land-based air units until the latter can be operated from shore" (*Tentative Manual for Landing Operations*: 12).

The manual described an infantry attack in the following phases: artillery preparation, movement forward, deployment in dispersed formation once within hostile weapons' ranges, and the final rush (with bayonets) to occupy enemy positions. In an amphibious assault, all but the last phase could occur while the landing craft approached the shore. This made operation and control of landing craft critical: "the leading troops must be quickly delivered in formation on the beach, deployed as skirmishers, or as near thereto as the small boats will permit. Supports and reserves must be maneuvered on the water so as to exploit successes ... all of the above phases up to the last rush take place while the attackers are on the water" (FTP-167: 62).

Troops and their landing craft were grouped in pairs. These included a landing group (usually a combat team built around a reinforced infantry battalion) and a boat group. Within these groups, specific landing elements such as reinforced platoons were paired with boat divisions of the boat group. These trained and rehearsed together so that on the day of the attack Marines and the sailors transporting them to the beach acted as a team. The men carried by a specific landing craft were designated a boat team and were organized to allow efficient use of landing-craft space. A boat team could be composed of a reinforced rifle squad, part of a rifle squad plus heavy-weapons' crews, medical, engineer, or other personnel. Once ashore, boat teams would reorganize into their normal units.

Controlling landing craft was both difficult and critically important for a successful landing. FTP-167 called for marking the line of departure with buoys or small boats, having a designated control vessel lead each boat group to the line of departure, guiding each wave of landing craft with wave and alternate wave guide boats, and having each boat display a letter and number identifying its position in the formation. Control vessels ranged from destroyers to small boats, depending on their assigned tasks.

The LCVP was 36ft long and 11ft wide. It was designed to be carried by transport and cargo ships from which it was hoisted into the water. It had a maximum speed of 12 knots and could carry either 36 men, or a jeep and 12 men, or 8,000lb of cargo. Its shallow draft (3ft aft and 2ft 2in forward) allowed it to run onto the shoreline. A steel ramp at the front could be lowered quickly to facilitate unloading. In the right conditions, the LCVP could rapidly unload its contents and return toward its parent ship in as little as three or four minutes, but still needed more water depth than that found at many Pacific landing beaches. (US Navy)

During the initial assault, a landing force's field-artillery batteries were on transport ships or landing craft waiting to get to shore. Therefore, ships' gunfire had to substitute:

> In amphibious operations, it is the mission of certain naval task groups to replace the landing force artillery in supporting the assaulting troops by fire on shore targets. That is, by delivering fire on enemy personnel, weapons, and other defensive installations, and on critical terrain features which may conceal undiscovered enemy positions, ship batteries enable the landing force first to land, then to advance, hold, or withdraw, with fewer casualties than would otherwise be possible. In some cases, effective naval gunfire may be the critical factor which determines success or failure.
>
> The fire support requirements of the infantry in an amphibious operation are essentially the same as the requirements in normal land warfare. The overall requirement may include fires executed in advance of D-day, such as bombardments for the destruction of enemy supplies and raids to confuse him as to the point of attack. The requirement may extend for some period of time beyond D-day in support of operations seeking to expand the beach head. If such is the case, plans must be made to effect resupply of ammunition. (FTP-167: 111)

Naval-gunfire support was structured around naval-gunfire "batteries," defined as two or more guns of the same caliber on the same ship controlled by the same fire-control station. The number of guns in a battery varied depending on the class of ship as did the number of batteries a given ship could form. Batteries were classed for four tactical purposes. These were (a) preparation – intensive fires delivered on the assault beaches and adjacent positions while the first wave of landing craft approached the beach; (b) close support – fires furnished in support of units ashore against enemy troops, weapons, or positions which were near the supported troops and posed the most immediate threat to them; (c) deep support – fires placed on enemy artillery, reserves, or critical points; and (d) special missions – deep supporting fires suited to use large-caliber naval guns against targets such as seacoast batteries and heavy permanent fortifications. Examples of naval-gunfire batteries given in FTP-167 included four 5in/25 guns for close support and

A pre-invasion briefing on an unidentified transport during the transit to Tarawa Atoll in November 1943. Large relief models were used to familiarize Marines and sailors with the topography of assault targets. These briefings were important to provide as much familiarization with the terrain as possible to men who had to orientate themselves and their units on a strange island and identify objectives while coming under enemy fire. (US Marine Corps)

six 6in/47 guns for close or deep support. Destroyers, with their 5in guns and small size, were a primary source of close-support batteries. Naval-gunfire support missions were a new role for warship captains.

Unity of command and teamwork were the keys to successful opposed amphibious operations. Doctrine called for a naval attack force to conduct an operation. Commanded by a senior naval officer, the naval attack force consisted of one or more naval task groups and the landing force of ground troops. Landing-force commanders embarked on the flagship with their US Navy counterparts throughout the chain of command to further teamwork. FTP-167 did not specify when the landing-force commander was to assume command of troops on shore. This, however, led to disagreements between US Navy and US Marine Corps officers several times during the Pacific War.

Constituent naval task groups could include reconnaissance groups, fire-support groups, air groups (sea- and land-based aircraft), transport groups, control groups (to manage the ship-to-shore movement), mine groups, salvage groups, and diversionary demonstration groups. Some groups would form for special tasks and then disband once these were completed, with the ships assigned to other groups. The landing force was organized into embarkation groups for loading aboard transports. Once ashore, troops would reorganize into their normal tactical units for extended land combat. Groups were created around regular tactical organizations such as regiments, battalions, and companies, with attachments and detachments as required.

Gas-mask-equipped SNLF troops pose for a photograph amid rubble in Shanghai, China, in 1937. Naval land operations in China provided the impetus for the creation of the SNLFs. The IJN needed semipermanent land units instead of temporary landing parties organized from ships' crews. Shanghai became home to the brigade-sized Shanghai SNLF, which survived intact until Japan's surrender in August 1945. Fighting the Chinese before 1941 earned the SNLF troops a reputation as a tough force, but one that was overrated in 1941 by the Western Allies. (Public Domain)

Japanese island defense doctrine

Japanese doctrine for island defense began with the IJN seeking to destroy an invasion force at sea. If this did not happen, Japanese defenders were to rely on coastal defense artillery to engage enemy ships and prevent a landing. If a landing occurred, the defenders were to destroy the enemy at the water's edge. If a landing force succeeded in establishing a beachhead, the defenders were to counterattack and destroy it. A wartime translation stated: "An island defense against a superior enemy lies in preventing the enemy from gaining a foothold on land by thoroughly prepared fortification, development of

Troops of the IJN's Special Naval Landing Forces (SNLFs) exercising with the 81mm Type 97 infantry mortar. The SNLFs used the same ground-combat equipment as the IJA. The SNLFs had a standard unit structure at platoon and company level, but above these, SNLFs could vary significantly in size and structure. Assigned weapons changed significantly during World War II as the SNLFs evolved from battalion-sized light-infantry assault units to heavily armed coastal defense forces. (Public Domain)

Infantryman, 7th Sasebo SNLF

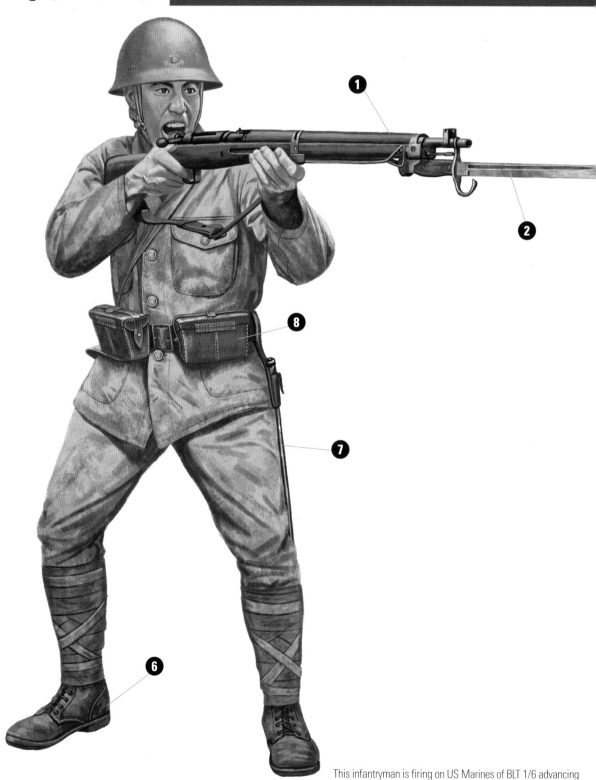

This infantryman is firing on US Marines of BLT 1/6 advancing toward the eastern end of Betio Island and the last of the Japanese defenses.

Weapons, dress, and equipment

He is armed with a 7.7mm Arisaka Type 99 bolt-action rifle (**1**). His Type 30 bayonet (**2**) with its 15½in blade is fixed: this is a suicidal charge and he is intent on killing as many Marines as he can.

He wears the SNLF 1933 summer uniform, consisting of a cotton jacket (**3**) and trousers (**4**). His helmet (**5**) is the IJN version of the Type 92 IJA helmet, which was of low grade and offered little in the way of protection from bullets or shell fragments. His Type 5 marching shoes (**6**) are made of horsehide and are hobnailed with

a metal-rimmed heel; the IJN version was made with smooth black leather and decayed quickly in the tropics.

His personal equipment includes a bayonet scabbard (**7**), two cartridge boxes (**8**) in the front each holding 30 rounds, and a larger cartridge box (**9**) worn in the rear holding 60 rounds (and a gun oil tube on the box's right side). His canteen (**10**), suspended from a web sling, is a Type 94 holding 2½ pints.

A damaged IJN twin 127mm Type 3 dual-purpose shore mount after the fighting. These guns, identical to those used on IJN surface ships, fired 51lb shells to a range of 20,100yd with a rate of fire of 5–10rd/min. Four twin mounts were on Betio Island (Tarawa Atoll), plus two twin mounts each on Kwajalein Atoll's Namur Island, Roi Island, and Kwajalein Island. Having a distinctive shape, the islands' 127mm batteries were targeted early by both air attacks and naval bombardment. (US Marine Corps)

massed firepower, and an assault on known ground. Consequently every effort must primarily be directed towards the strengthening of the fortifications" (MISLS: 3). To counter US firepower, the Japanese knew they needed strong man-made fortifications:

> Against an enemy who utilizes an enormous amount of materiel for his combat power we must first construct a formidable fortification in such a way as to prevent the full use of the enemy's equipment, thereby dispersing or limiting his fierce fire power. It is also important to prevent him from using tanks etc. For this reason it is the paramount duty of a garrison unit to build an invulnerable island fortress by

The IJN used the 80mm Type 41 naval gun as both an anti-landing and antiaircraft weapon. This photo shows an example emplacement on Makin Atoll in the Gilberts. The Type 41, based on a British design from 1893 and manufactured under license in Japan, was actually a 3in (76.2mm) gun, but designated as 80mm by the IJN. It fired a round weighing approximately 13lb to an effective range of 18,000yd with a rate of fire of 13–20rd/min. (US Army)

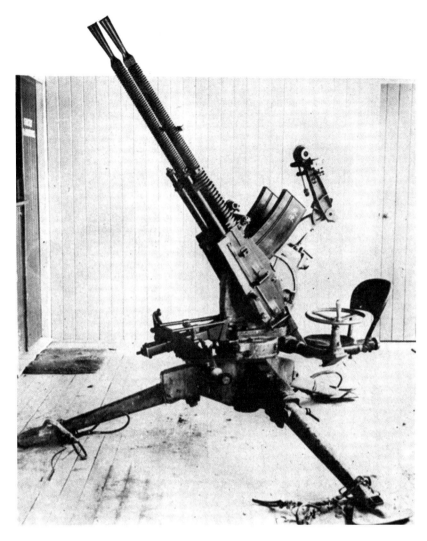

Used afloat and ashore, the IJN's 13mm Type 93 antiaircraft machine gun came in three forms: single mount, twin mount, and quadruple mount. The gun was a Hotchkiss design that was built under license in Japan. Its range was 6,560yd with an effective antiaircraft engagement altitude of 13,000ft, but the 30-round magazine restricted its rate of fire to 250rd/min. (NARA)

using all available material, and carry on construction with ceaseless efforts until the enemy has commenced landing. (MISLS: 4)

Defending units and all other personnel on an island were expected to fight to the death, either defeating the Americans or dying in the attempt to do so:

> ... on an isolated island, it is essential that the entire personnel down to the last man, be imbued completely with the belief in certain victory, and invincibility, and become thoroughly instilled with the bold fighting spirit of self sacrifice and destruction of the enemy in battle. They must sacrifice themselves for the glory of the history of Imperial Japan which has existed for 3,000 years. (MISLS: 3)

The IJN's Combined Fleet was unable to challenge the US Fifth Fleet during the Gilberts and Marshalls operations. Japanese garrisons were left to fight on their own. If they failed to repel an enemy landing, they were to sacrifice their lives for the Japanese Empire while inflicting as many losses as possible on their enemy.

RECRUITMENT AND FORCE STRUCTURE

US Marine Corps

By 1943 Marines were volunteers or, after December 5, 1942, draftees who volunteered to join the US Marine Corps during their draft induction. This resulted in Marine riflemen being of higher quality than those in normal US Army infantry divisions. This difference was because US Army rifle companies were assigned those draftees remaining after the US Army Air Forces and other technical branches had selected personnel. Considering themselves "volunteers" gave the Marines a high *esprit de corps.* This resulted in greater aggressiveness, initiative, and unit cohesion.

The US Marine Corps used the Series E Table of Organization during the Gilberts and Marshalls operations. The Series E Marine division was composed of three infantry regiments, one artillery regiment, one engineer regiment, one tank battalion, one special-weapons battalion, one amphibian tractor battalion, one medical battalion, one transportation battalion, and one service battalion. Divisions numbered 19,965 men, consisting of 908 Marine and 133 Navy officers along with 17,236 Marine and 1,688 Navy enlisted men. Series E divisions were armed with 11,074 .30-caliber M1 Garand semiautomatic rifles, 558 .30-caliber Browning Automatic Rifles, 682 .30-caliber light (air-cooled) machine guns, 108 .30-caliber heavy (water-cooled) machine guns, 313 .50-caliber heavy machine guns, 54 37mm antitank guns, 12 75mm self-propelled antitank guns, 36 75mm and 24 105mm howitzers, 162 mortars (half 60mm and half 81mm), and 54 light tanks armed with a 37mm main gun.

Marine regiments were numbered in sequence from the 1st through 29th. By the end of the Pacific War, there were 18 Marine infantry regiments, numbered 1st–9th and 21st–29th. Six Marine artillery regiments were numbered 10th–15th while the 16th–20th Marines were engineer regiments.

Marines debark from ships' boats during an early landing exercise. The lack of purpose-designed landing craft initially forced the use of ships' boats for landing, just as the lack of purpose-built transports required older battleships to be used as transports. During 1935–41 a regular series of Fleet Landing Exercises (FLEXs) were conducted by the US Navy, the US Marine Corps, and the US Army. FLEX 1 saw the Wyoming-class battleships USS *Arkansas* (BB-33) and USS *Wyoming* (BB-32) used as transports and 18 ships' boats and one unpowered lighter employed as landing craft. FLEXs refined doctrine, tested new equipment, and developed tactics, leading to successful amphibious operations in World War II. (US Marine Corps)

Marines debarking from an LVT-2 under fire on Namur Island, Kwajalein Atoll. The LVT was designed as a ship-to-shore supply carrier but also was used to carry assault troops across coral reefs beginning at Tarawa Atoll. The LVT-2 had a better engine and was more reliable than the LVT-1. The LVT-2 could carry 24 fully equipped Marines or 6,500lb of payload. It could travel at 6.2mph in water and 20mph on land. Machine guns could be fitted behind the driver's cab, along the sides, and at the rear of the troop/cargo space. LVTs were usually conveyed to the assault area in a Landing Ship Tank (LST) from which they could drive into the water. (US Navy)

All regiments were called "Marine." Divisional battalions were numbered with the parent division's number, e.g. the 2d Tank Battalion was organic to the 2d Marine Division. The 2d Marine Division included the following regiments: 2d, 6th, 8th (all infantry); 10th (artillery); and 18th (engineer). The 4th Marine Division's regiments were: 23d, 24th, 25th (all infantry); 14th (artillery); and 20th (engineer).

A division's tank battalion included a scout company and three tank companies of five platoons, each equipped with three light tanks. Because the light tanks' 37mm main gun was inadequate for overcoming Japanese field fortifications, M4A2 medium tanks were added to the Gilberts and Marshalls operations. The special-weapons battalion included a 40mm antiaircraft battery and three antitank batteries equipped with 37mm towed antitank guns and 75mm self-propelled guns (on halftracks). Amphibian tractor battalions had a Headquarters & Service (H&S) company (with ten LVTs) and three companies, each with 27 LVTs. The number of LVTs varied depending on the operation.

Series E infantry regiments (3,242 officers and men) included one H&S company, one regimental weapons company, and three infantry battalions. The H&S company included a scout-sniper platoon and US Navy aid station. Regimental weapons companies had three antitank platoons, each with four 37mm antitank guns, and a fourth platoon with two 75mm self-propelled guns. Infantry battalions consisted of a headquarters company, a weapons company, and three rifle companies. Companies were designated by letters (A, B, C, etc.) within the regiment, but the letter "J" was never used to designate a company.

An artillery regiment had five battalions; three with M1A1 75mm pack howitzers and two with M2A1 105mm howitzers. Each battalion had three firing batteries each equipped with four howitzers. In the Marshalls, the 14th Marines (4th Marine Division) had only four battalions, two 75mm and two 105mm. Batteries were designated by letters as in the infantry companies.

Engineer regiments had three battalions. The 1st Battalion was a combat-engineer unit with three companies that provided specialized demolition and assault capabilities. The 2d Battalion was a pioneer unit of three companies used in the shore party for unloading landing craft and moving supplies; they also provided construction services and were trained and armed like infantry. The 3d Battalion was a US Navy Naval Construction Battalion that performed construction ranging from airstrips and roads to fuel-storage facilities and pipelines.

The separate 22d Marines fought on Eniwetok Atoll. This was a series E infantry regiment with attachments making it a standalone combined-arms team. Attached were a 75mm pack howitzer battalion, a tank company, an engineer company, a transport company, and a medical company.

Marines organized combined-arms teams for assault landings and combat. An infantry regiment would have attached artillery battalions, tank companies, engineer companies, and service and support detachments. An infantry regiment plus attachments went by several names: Regimental Combat Team (RCT), Regimental Landing Team (RLT), or Combat Team (CT). The 2d Marine Division used "CT" on Tarawa (e.g. the 6th Marines reinforced was CT6), while the 4th Marine Division used "RCT" on Roi-Namur (e.g. the 24th Marines reinforced was RCT24).

The landing group of FTP-167's "landing group/boat group" pair was usually a "battalion landing team" (BLT). A BLT was a reinforced infantry battalion. FTP-167 gave an early-war example of a BLT to explain landing groups and boat groups and how to calculate the number of landing-craft boat spaces that were needed. This BLT example consisted of one infantry battalion, one 75mm pack howitzer battery, one artillery reconnaissance detachment, one tank platoon, one antitank platoon from the regimental weapons company, one engineer platoon, and detachments for shore- and beach-party duties. The BLT was in effect a combined-arms slice of its parent division.

Amphibious-assault task organization extended to the lowest level, which was an individual landing craft and the "boat team" it carried. FTP-167 showed a notional division of four landing craft carrying a reinforced prewar

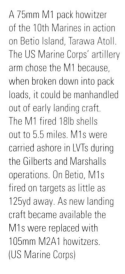

A 75mm M1 pack howitzer of the 10th Marines in action on Betio Island, Tarawa Atoll. The US Marine Corps' artillery arm chose the M1 because, when broken down into pack loads, it could be manhandled out of early landing craft. The M1 fired 18lb shells out to 5.5 miles. M1s were carried ashore in LVTs during the Gilberts and Marshalls operations. On Betio, M1s fired on targets as little as 125yd away. As new landing craft became available the M1s were replaced with 105mm M2A1 howitzers. (US Marine Corps)

During 1943–44, the US Marine Corps used the diesel-powered M4A2 medium tank in the Pacific. The M4A2 weighed just over 35 tons and carried a five-man crew; it was armed with a 75mm main gun, one .50-caliber antiaircraft machine gun atop the turret, and two .30-caliber machine guns, one coaxial with the 75mm main gun and one hull mounted in front. At first, one company in each tank battalion (designated on paper as "light") was equipped with the M4. Later, Marine tank battalions as a whole were equipped with the M4. (US Army)

rifle platoon in four boat teams. Boat 1 carried the platoon commander, message runners, one rifle squad, and attached machine-gunners; boat 2 carried one rifle squad, attached machine-gunners, and medical corpsmen; boat 3 had the same load as boat 2; and boat 4 carried a platoon sergeant, one message runner, one automatic-rifle squad, and attached machine-gunners. This reinforced platoon totaled 58 men. As Marine tables of organization changed and new landing craft, and LVTs, carried the assault troops, the organization of boat teams was adapted. The goal was a team capable of fighting immediately upon debarking from its landing craft.

Japanese forces

IJN ground troops in the Gilberts and Marshalls were a mix of trained ground units (SNLFs, SBFs, and Guard Units) and construction (mostly civilian laborers), supply, administration, maintenance, and aviation ground crews. All sailors stationed on an invaded atoll or island were expected to fight to the death according to the Japanese military ethos. With rudimentary training, a man armed with a light machine gun and determined to die fighting could be a formidable opponent. This ethos forced US troops to close the final yards to capture that position.

The IJN originally had marines similar to those of Britain's Royal Navy, but these were disbanded in 1876 and replaced by naval landing forces organized on an ad hoc basis from ships' crews. These sailors served as infantry or artillery once ashore. All sailors received basic infantry and ground-warfare training as part of their primary training syllabus. Training was done at the IJN's four Naval Districts named after the four major IJN bases: Kure, Sasebo, Yokosuka, and Maizuru. Ships' landing forces were used during the Satsuma Rebellion (1876). Subsequently, ships' landing forces saw action during the First Sino-Japanese War (1894–95), the Boxer Rebellion in China (1899–1901), and the Russo-Japanese War (1904–05). When Japanese naval landing forces joined the Allies against Imperial Germany in 1914, they were used in the attack on German-held Tsingtao and captured German-held islands in the Central Pacific (including the Marshalls). Landing forces were used in Siberia at the start of the Japanese intervention during the Russian Civil War (1917–22). Once a mission was completed the sailors returned to their ships and the landing force was disbanded. The problem with this practice was that ships' crews were depleted and ships' efficiencies were reduced while their sailors were ashore.

When fighting in China flared up in the 1920s, the IJN provided landing forces from ships' crews. The demand for naval ground forces in China led to the formation of semipermanent units using sailors not assigned to ships' companies. These units were first used in Shanghai in 1927 to reinforce, and then replace, ships' landing forces. These units became part of the new Shanghai Naval Landing Force. This command grew to brigade size but was reduced to battalion size after fighting around Shanghai had died down. The renewal of fighting around Shanghai in 1937 led to an expansion of IJN ground forces. Naval Districts were ordered to raise battalion-sized units named Specially Designated Naval District Special Naval Landing Forces (*Rikusentai*; more commonly called SNLFs in English). Units were designated by a number and the forming district/base name, such as 1st Sasebo SNLF or 3d Kure SNLF. The first SNLFs raised were used in China. During 1937–40, 19 units were formed – 1st–4th Yokosuka, 1st–6th Kure, and 1st–9th Sasebo – all but two of which were disbanded or incorporated into other units (e.g. the Shanghai Naval Landing Force) by 1941. The two SNLFs left active (4th Yokosuka and 8th Sasebo) fought Chinese guerrillas on Hainan Island and remained there until Japan's surrender in 1945. In June 1940 the 1st Maizuru SNLF was raised and sent to Hainan Island where it too remained until Japan's surrender. The combat performance of these early SNLFs was assessed in a US War Department 1944 report: "Their performance was excellent when unopposed, but when determined resistance was encountered they exhibited a surprising lack of ability in infantry combat" (TM-E-30-480: 76).

Beginning in November 1940 new SNLFs were organized for the impending Pacific War, many reusing the designations of units previously disbanded in China. By November 1941 there were eight new SNLFs; two were parachute units and six were conventional coastal landing units. The parachute units, the 1st and 3d Yokosuka SNLFs, had a special structure. The other six – 2d Yokosuka, 1st and 2d Sasebo, 1st and 2d Kure, and 2d Maizuru SNLFs – were infantry units the nominal formation of which was based on a 1939 structure of three rifle companies, one artillery company, a headquarters, and support units. Personnel totaled 42 officers and 1,158 other ranks.

In practice, the 1939 structure was only used as a general guide; each SNLF was tailored as needed. Strengths of the SNLFs ranged from the 742-man 2d Yokosuka SNLF to the 1,612-man 1st Sasebo SNLF. In November 1941, the 2d Maizuru SNLF had 1,071 men. This was the only SNLF in the Central Pacific at the start of the Pacific War and part of it participated in the capture of Wake Island in December 1942. SNLFs played a role in Japan's initial offensives. A 1944 US War Department publication stated:

> When the present war began, special naval landing forces at first were used to occupy a chain of Pacific island bases. Wake Island was taken by one such force, while another seized the Gilbert Islands. Later they were used to spearhead landing operations against Java, Ambon, and Rabaul, where the bulk of the attack forces consisted of army personnel. During this period the special naval landing forces, although heavily armed, were used as mobile striking units. (TM-E-30-480: 76)

Once their offensive missions were completed, SNLFs were frequently disbanded, as illustrated by their wartime fates. The parachute-trained 1st and 3d Yokosuka SNLFs were consolidated into the 1st Yokosuka SNLF in December 1942 and did not see further combat until June 1944, when the unit was destroyed on Saipan. By April 1942 all six non-parachute prewar SNLFs had been converted to garrisons and guards in newly conquered territories. Between February 1942 and June 1943, 15 new SNLFs were raised for the Pacific War, but most of these had short lifespans. Three of these survived as SNLFs in isolated garrisons, the rest were disbanded, converted to Guard Units or SBFs, or destroyed in combat. Additional SNLFs were raised in Japan for home defense near the end of the war using whatever manpower was available.

The IJN considered SNLFs as naval personnel assigned to temporary duties onshore and assignment to them was not popular. Units were manned with lower categories of conscripts and reservists. New SNLFs were not formed by expanding veteran units; instead, Naval Districts organized these from scratch when ordered to provide a unit. Fresh conscripts and mobilized reservists comprised the bulk of SNLF personnel. Although men with ground-combat experience were placed in new SNLFs when available as a cadre, their manpower was generally inexperienced in land warfare. In 1944, American intelligence stated that:

> ... earlier special naval landing forces received extensive training in landing operations and beach defense, but their training in infantry weapons and tactics does not appear to have been up to the standard of the Japanese Army. More recently there has been a greater emphasis on infantry training for units already in existence. Tactical doctrine for land warfare follows that of the Army, with certain changes based on lessons learned during the current war. The platoon is the basic tactical unit, rather than the company. (TM-E-30-480: 78)

Lieutenant Charles Gerard, Sergeant Marshall Epling, Sergeant Harold Harper, Private First Class Robert Hasman, and Sergeant Raymond Mieure from the 1st Raider Battalion, US Marine Corps, use a captured 37mm Type 94 antitank gun to fire on Japanese positions at Cape Torokina in Empress Augusta Bay during the Solomon Islands campaign, November 1943. (Keystone/Hulton Archive/Getty Images)

Despite their shortcomings, the SNLFs gained a reputation as fearsome fighters from their early successes during the offensives of 1941–42. They retained this reputation through stubborn defensive actions in the Pacific during 1942–44, frequently fighting to the last man and last bullet.

IJN Guard Units were formed by Naval Districts or sometimes in the field to provide land defense for fixed naval bases and installations. Guard Units were usually designated with a number (e.g. 61st Naval Guard Unit), but a few in China and on prewar Japanese-controlled islands were named (e.g., Iwo Jima Guard Unit). Guard Units did not have a standard size and organization; instead, they were structured as needed for their specific location and duties. Their ground-combat training was analogous to that given SNLFs. Personnel strengths varied from a few hundred to several thousand men. Guard Units included a ground security branch (organized similarly to the SNLF), a maritime security branch, and a supply branch. The tactical organization was fluid and tailored to specific tasks. During the first year of the Pacific War some Guard Units organized landing forces to secure small objectives and undefended islands. The 61st Naval Guard Unit, which started the war with 557 men, was stationed on Kwajalein Atoll. This unit, structured around coastal defense and antiaircraft guns, was expanded to 1,900 men by January 1944.

Construction battalions were independent mobile units for major construction projects. Each was designated with a number and its manpower included eight officers, one warrant officer, 92 enlisted (including petty officers), 415 workmen (skilled), and 1,045 laborers (mostly conscripted Koreans). After the completion of

The Japanese made extensive use of the Model 89 grenade discharger, mistakenly called a knee mortar. It was a muzzle-loaded rifled weapon firing a 50mm high-explosive round weighing 1.25lb out to a range of 737yd. The discharger weighed 10lb and was able to be brought into action quickly. The weapon was braced against any convenient object, but not the firer's knee as the powerful recoil could break the firer's kneecap and thigh bone. These weapons were liberally supplied to IJA and IJN ground troops. (US Marine Corps)

training under Naval Districts, construction battalions were assigned to fleets (e.g. 4th Fleet in the Gilberts and Marshalls). They were then assigned to Base Forces, SBFs, and Guard Units. Construction battalions, which were supervised by IJN civilian engineers and IJN officers, worked closely with other IJN construction units such as Fleet Construction Departments. All IJN personnel received basic infantry training and could (and did) fight as infantry when needed; and skilled workmen, some of whom had prior military training, were pressed into service in island battles. The Korean laborers were used to carry supplies, dig fortifications, and conduct noncombat service activities. Koreans accounted for the majority of prisoners-of-war captured from Japanese units in the Pacific.

IJN Base Forces and Special Base Forces (SBFs) were responsible for advanced naval bases in forward areas. A Base Force was originally intended to be a commanding headquarters for noncombatant support units deployed to forward bases. These were generally small headquarters – administrative units – and seldom had any combat role. Subordinates to a Base Force could include Guard Units, depots, construction, communications, maintenance, and transportation units. An SBF combined these functions with tactical defense duties. The 3d SBF was responsible for defending the Gilberts. It commanded the Tarawa Atoll garrison (including the 7th Sasebo SNLF), the Makin Atoll garrison (a detachment of the 3d SBF), the Nauru Island garrison, and the Ocean Island garrison (the last two composed of the 2d Yokosuka SNLF and 67th Guard Unit). By January 1944 the 6th Base Force (headquarters on Kwajalein Island) commanded six Guard Units on atolls in the Marshalls and one on Wake Atoll. It also commanded the 6th Submarine Base Unit, 14th Torpedo Maintenance Section, 106th Air Depot, and detachments of the 4th Fleet Maintenance Division, 4th Fleet Account and Supply Division, and 4th Fleet Construction Division.

Noncombat personnel were organized as improvised infantry when an island they were stationed on was invaded. On Roi-Namur the ground elements of the IJN's 24th Air Flotilla were used to form the Yamada Unit under Rear Admiral Yamada Michiyuki, the 24th Air Flotilla commander. The unit was composed of pilots without aircraft, aircraft mechanics, and other aviation support personnel. All sailors had basic infantry training and could operate rifles and light machine guns. Sometimes machine guns were stripped from wrecked aircraft and used as improvised infantry weapons.

US forces encountered a new type of IJA unit in the Marshalls, which was the amphibious (or sea-mobile) brigade. The IJA created amphibious brigades beginning in November 1943, 23 months after the attack on Pearl Harbor. Four of these were formed during the Pacific War. The 1st Amphibious Brigade, organized in November 1943 from the 3d Independent Garrison Unit in Manchuria, was sent to the Marshalls in January 1944 (minus its sea transport engineer regiment) and was mostly destroyed in the fighting on Eniwetok except for elements isolated on bypassed atolls (the brigade was divided between Eniwetok, Kwajalein, Wotje, and Maloelap atolls). The 2d Amphibious Brigade was sent to western New Guinea and was stranded there as the war moved farther on. The 3d and 4th Amphibious brigades remained in the Home Islands.

An amphibious brigade was structured to reduce the amount of shipping required to move it. Land transportation was limited and once offloaded, the brigade's personnel moved on foot. It had no field artillery; its weapons were all man-portable. On paper, an IJA sea transport engineer regiment with motorized landing barges was attached.

The core of an amphibious brigade was three 1,030-man battalions. These were combined-arms teams each of which had a pioneer platoon, three rifle companies, one mortar company, and one artillery company. The rifle companies were consecutively numbered (e.g. 3d Battalion rifle companies were the 7th, 8th, and 9th) while mortar and artillery companies were named, e.g. Mortar Company 1st Battalion. The amphibious brigade had a headquarters company, a brigade engineer company, a tank company with nine Type 95 Ha-Gō light tanks, a machine-cannon company with six 20mm automatic guns, a supply company, and a medical company. Although other IJA units were stationed in the Marshalls, US Marines did not encounter them.

Like the IJA, the SNLFs employed the 70mm Type 92 howitzer – shown here in US hands – as a battalion-level infantry-support weapon, and it proved to be very effective. When broken down it could be man-packed, which made it very useful for SNLF units during amphibious landings. It fired a shell weighing approximately 10lb to an effective range of 3,060yd with a rate of fire of 10rd/min. US Marines frequently reported they were taking mortar fire when in fact they were being shelled by Type 92 infantry guns. Like that of the IJA, the 1939 SNLF "battalion howitzer platoon" was equipped with two guns. (US Marine Corps)

Betio Island, Tarawa Atoll

November 20–23, 1943

BACKGROUND TO BATTLE

On September 15, 1942, the 6th Yokosuka SNLF landed on Tarawa Atoll followed by the IJN's 111th Construction Unit in December. The 6th Yokosuka SNLF was redesignated the 3d SBF on February 15, 1943, and subsequently converted into a coastal defense unit. In March 1943 the 7th Sasebo SNLF was attached to the 3d SBF. After he became commander of 3d SBF on July 20, 1943, Rear Admiral Shibasaki Keiji

> ... established a new program by enforcing military discipline and training. On Tarawa, from dawn till dusk the men underwent rigid training. As a result of this

A pair of British-made 8in Vickers turret-mounted coastal guns on Betio Island. Postwar assertions that the four guns installed on Betio were captured at Singapore were mistaken – they had been purchased by Japan from Vickers in 1905 during the Russo-Japanese War (1904–05). Their size made them obvious targets for air strikes and naval bombardment. In the end, they proved of little value to Betio's defenders. (US Marine Corps)

intense training, which was conducted for a period of four months from the day of Admiral Shibazaki's [*sic*] arrival to the day of the enemy's attack, their strength was improved tremendously with the resulting psychological lift to the men. (SDB 1952)

By November 1943, Tarawa Atoll's defenses included: eight 8in, eight 140mm, and six 80mm coastal defense guns; four twin 127mm dual-purpose gun mounts, and eight 75mm antiaircraft guns. There were ten 75mm mountain howitzers, six 70mm infantry guns, nine 37mm antitank pieces, at least 27 single and four dual 13mm antiaircraft machine guns, and 14 Type 95 Ha-Gō light tanks. Japanese manpower on Tarawa Atoll was: 3d SBF (less detachments elsewhere), 902; 7th Sasebo SNLF, 1,669; 111th Construction Unit, 2,000; aviation, 30 – a total of 4,601 officers and men.

Shibasaki planned to destroy any attacker at the water's edge. Coastal guns were ordered to destroy enemy transports. Mountain guns, infantry guns, antitank guns, and machine guns were to engage approaching landing craft. Beach defenses relied on

> ... the 13mm machine gun, supplemented by the 7.7mm machine gun. These were sited to cover most likely approaches to the beach with frontal fire, and to cover the forward side of the diagonally placed barriers on the reef with flanking fires, these fires interlocking in front of, and protecting, other beach defense weapon installations. Carefully built rifle and light machine-gun emplacements were positioned in the log beach barricade and immediately behind it to provide local protection for automatic fire weapons. (Stockman 1947: 8)

Mines were laid on the beach and fringing coral reef. A double-apron barbed-wire fence encircled the island 50–100yd from the beach. Anti-boat obstacles were built, "the purpose of which was twofold: (1) To slow down and otherwise impede the movements of landing craft; (2) to force approaching landing craft into prearranged fire lanes where concentrated fires from all types of

Film from a Japanese camera found on Betio shows SNLF personnel at target practice in 1943 sometime before the US attack. The IJN defenders trained intensively in the months beforehand – note the large number of light machine guns in use. The Marines could not establish the exact number of Japanese light machine guns that had been in use on Betio because many were destroyed and buried as a result of the intensive air and naval bombardment. (US Marine Corps)

weapons could be employed most advantageously" (Stockman 1947: 8). The fortifications were a hard shell built around a soft core: "Defenses inland were haphazard. Command posts, ammunition dumps, and communication centers were made of reinforced concrete and were virtually bombproof. They were not purposely constructed as positions from which active resistance could be offered" (Stockman 1947: 8). Because the defenses were heavily oriented to the ocean side of Betio, by landing on the lagoon side, the Marines encountered weaker, but still formidable, defenses.

Capturing Tarawa Atoll was assigned to the 2d Marine Division, commanded by Major General Julian C. Smith. The division was organized into three combat teams: CT2 (2d Marines reinforced), CT6 (6th Marines reinforced), and CT8 (8th Marines reinforced). CT2, with BLT 2/8 attached, was the assault force. The assault landed three BLTs (3/2, 2/2, and 2/8) abreast west to east on beaches designated Red 1, Red 2, and Red 3. CT2's reserve was BLT 1/2. CT8 (less BLT 2/8) was divisional reserve, and CT6 was V Amphibious Corps' (VAC) reserve, to be used only with Corps' approval. The 2d Marine Division had wanted to capture islets on which to deploy its artillery before D-day, but this was rejected on grounds that it would give more time for IJN air and submarine attacks against US Navy ships.

Assault troops had to cross the coral reef to get to the three beaches. Landing craft (LCVPs and LCMs) needed 4ft of water to operate, but sailors with experience of the Gilberts estimated water depths over the reef varied from insufficient to adequate. The 2d Marine Division therefore decided to convert LVTs for use as assault-troop carriers, and 75 LVT-1s were duly modified with extemporized armor and additional machine guns. On D-day, 50 new LVT-2s from Hawaii joined the division at sea. With three assault battalions to transport the 125 LVTs could carry the first three waves, leaving the fourth and fifth waves to be transported in landing craft.

The northwestern tip of Betio, viewed from a US observation aircraft. The south shore of the island is visible in the top of the photograph. To left stretches Red Beach where the D-day landings took place. On the right is Green Beach, over which battalions of the 6th Marines landed without opposition during the evening of D+1 and D+2. The presence of LVTs on the beach in the foreground gives one an impression of the small size of the island. (US Navy)

1 **0910hrs, November 20:** BLT 3/2 in LVTs lands on Red 1.

2 **0917hrs, November 20:** BLT 2/8 in LVTs lands on Red 3.

3 **0922hrs, November 20:** BLT 2/2 in LVTs lands on Red 2.

4 **0958hrs, November 20:** BLT 1/2 is ordered to land on Red 2. Two companies go ashore in LVTs; the remainder have to wade ashore under heavy fire.

5 **1103hrs, November 20:** BLT 3/8 is ordered to land on Red 3 using LCVPs and LCMs. Forced to wade ashore under fire, its landing is not completed until around 1730hrs.

6 **0615hrs, November 21:** BLT 1/8 and CT8's command group begin landing on Red 2. Wading across 500yd of coral reef, they suffer heavy casualties.

7 **1120hrs, November 21:** Elements of BLT 3/2, with tank support, attack toward the south shore of Betio to clear Green Beach.

8 **1225hrs, November 21:** Green Beach is declared secured; BLT 3/2 turns east and sets up defenses.

9 **1300hrs, November 21:** BLT 1/2 and BLT 2/2 attack across the airstrip toward the south shore.

10 **1800–1835hrs, November 21:** BLT 1/6 lands unopposed on Green Beach South using rubber boats to cross the reef.

11 **0805hrs, November 22:** BLT 1/6 launches a full-strength battalion attack toward the east, supported by one M4A2 medium tank and seven M3A1 light tanks.

12 **0805hrs, November 22:** Elements of BLT 3/2 simultaneously attack north of the airstrip toward the east.

13 **1015hrs, November 22:** BLT 1/6 gains visual contact with CT2 on the south shore of Betio; 45 minutes later, physical contact is established.

14 **1330hrs, November 22:** After resting and reorganizing, Co. A, 6th Marines, and supporting tanks continue the US attack eastward.

15 **1800hrs, November 22:** Co. A, 6th Marines, is moved across the airstrip to a night-defense position on the north shore; the remainder of BLT 1/6 digs in south of the airstrip for the night, with Co. B, 6th Marines, holding the front line.

16 **0400hrs, November 23:** About 300 IJN troops charge all along the front of Co. B, 6th Marines, and the right of Co. A, 6th Marines. The attack is repulsed with heavy Japanese losses.

17 **0800hrs, November 23:** BLT 3/6 attacks through BLT 1/6's lines.

18 **1310hrs, November 23:** BLT 3/6 reaches the eastern tip of Betio.

Battlefield environment

Tarawa Atoll is located near 1°20′N, 173°00′E, and has a lagoon measuring 193 square miles with coral-reef openings for large ships. Fighting was concentrated on heavily fortified Betio Island at the southwest corner of the atoll. Betio is shaped like a long, thin triangle and is about 2 miles long but only 800yd at its widest point. The island is relatively flat; its highest elevation is 10ft.

The atoll and island have an equatorial climate and experience high mean annual temperatures, small temperature ranges, and year-round rainfall. November's average high temperature is 88.3°F with relative humidity of 79 percent. These combine to give a heat index (the heat the human body feels) of 107°F. Men fighting and working in this climate required large amounts of drinking water to stay hydrated and not suffer heat prostration. Natural water supply is limited to underground water, which tends to be brackish. The Japanese relied on stored water for their troops while the Americans supplied water from ships' freshwater distillation systems in containers transported by landing craft to the men ashore.

Like most atoll islands, Betio's soil is of poor quality and threatened by erosion. It is rocky and sandy, making digging difficult. Explosions threw up coral-rock fragments, which could inflict serious wounds and even death.

The airfield dominated the ground on Betio. The runway, taxiways, and dispersal area created a large, clear, level, and unfortified area that provided clear fields of fire for both defender and attacker. US tanks and halftracks were easily able to maneuver on its surface.

On the southern (ocean) side of Betio the reef was about 600yd from the island. Here the open sea caused heavy swells that could swamp small boats. Off the western beaches the currents were strong and unpredictable. On the lagoon side of the island the reef was wide and rose gradually to the surface. Betio formed a natural breakwater, which resulted in smoother waters and lower waves inside the lagoon. Large ships could anchor inside the lagoon. Men and materiel were transferred between these and the island by small craft. Betio's long pier reached beyond the reef into the lagoon and serviced smaller sized craft that traveled between atolls.

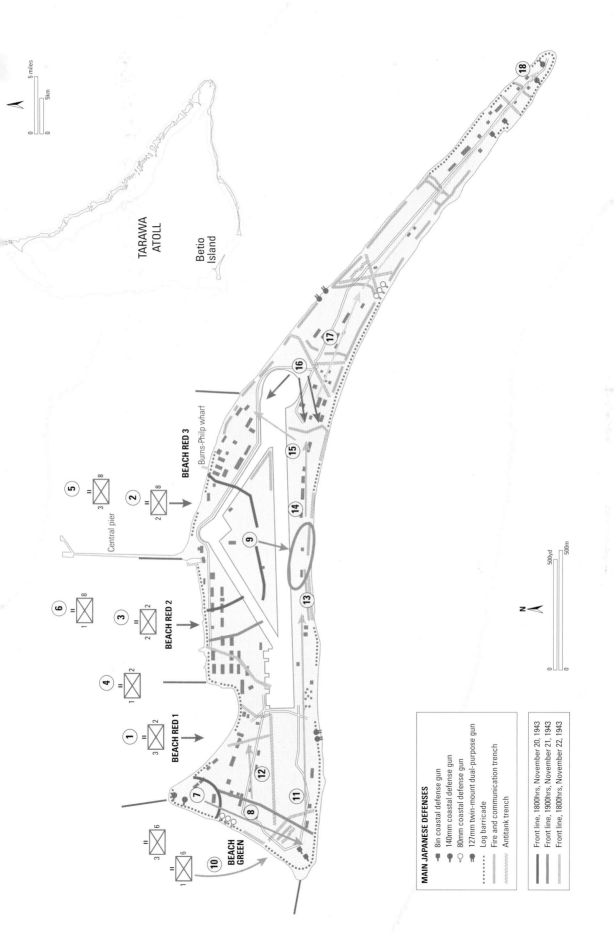

TARAWA ATOLL

Betio Island

5 miles
5km

BEACH RED 3

Burns-Philp wharf

Central pier

BEACH RED 2

BEACH RED 1

BEACH GREEN

500yd
500m

N

MAIN JAPANESE DEFENSES

⊩	8in coastal defense gun
⊩	140mm coastal defense gun
⦵	80mm coastal defense gun
⦷	127mm twin-mount dual-purpose gun
⋯⋯	Log barricade
	Fire and communication trench
▨▨	Antitank trench

▬	Front line, 1800hrs, November 20, 1943
▬	Front line, 1900hrs, November 21, 1943
▬	Front line, 1800hrs, November 22, 1943

INTO COMBAT

About 3,000 tons of shells were fired on Betio Island, mostly in the hours preceding the landings. At 0855hrs, November 20, the shelling ceased, except for that of two US Navy destroyers in the lagoon east of the landing beaches that could see Betio and the assault waves. These destroyers fired until 0910hrs when the first LVTs (carrying BLT 3/2) landed on Red 1. The LVTs carrying BLT 2/8 landed on Red 3 at 0917hrs and those carrying BLT 2/2 landed on Red 2 at 0922hrs. Air and naval bombardment was not as effective as expected, however. The US Marine Corps' postwar assessment stated:

> The firing of the support ships prior to H-hour was excellent, as far as it went. The coast defense guns on Betio were silent, the guns destroyed or their crews killed. Most of the dual purpose antiaircraft guns were neutralized. Many of the anti boat guns were out of action. Unfortunately, however, few of the smaller beach defense guns and pillboxes were destroyed. The machine guns, some of the 37mm anti boat guns, and emplacements holding riflemen were still operative ... (Stockman 1947: 13–14)

Serious Japanese resistance began after the first three LVT-transported assault waves reached their designated beaches. Marines began to suffer significant casualties only after debarking from their LVTs when a log barricade erected by the Japanese defenders prevented them from advancing inland. Captain Warren Morris, commanding Co. F, 2d Marines, described the assault:

> I landed in the first wave at about 0905, receiving heavy fire by the time we hit the beach. We were supposed to land in the middle of the company area at about the right flank of 220 [map grid], but instead we landed in the right flank of 222 [map grid]. I got ashore with myself and four out of the eighteen who started. We had two flame throwers in the first wave, neither of which got ashore, but we did get demolition kits in ...
>
> About H+60, I got 15 men from Company "E" in charge of a Sergeant. He did not know where the officers were. About 1200 part of 1-2 came in. We attached a mortar squad to them, and they pushed forward receiving only sniper fire ...
>
> We continued around the right flank to form a perimeter defense. We had about 30 wounded there, and a Doctor and some Corpsmen set up an aid station on the beach. We had little trouble that night. Late on D Day I found my Exec and 25 men left of the Company. (Quoted in FMFRP 12-90: 41–42)

Waves 4 and 5 in LCVPs and LCMs were stopped by shallow water over the coral reef. These Marines had to wade ashore for up to 500yd over the reef while coming under heavy fire from Japanese defenders. The battalions' command groups, heavy weapons, 75mm pack howitzers, and tanks (both light and medium) were in these two waves. Heavy weapons were frequently lost on the reef and the assault battalions became further disorganized.

At 0958hrs, Colonel David M. Shoup ordered BLT 1/2 to land, but only enough LVTs were gathered to carry two companies. It was not until early on D+1 that this battalion was fully ashore. At 1103hrs Division then ordered BLT 3/8 to land and reinforce CT2 on Red 3 using LCVPs and LCMs.

Forced to wade ashore under fire, the battalion suffered heavy casualties and only completed its landing around 1730hrs. At 1130hrs, 14 M4A2 medium tanks transported in LCMs started landing. As the tanks drove over the reef, however, two fell into reef craters. The M3A1 light tanks had less wading capability, which meant they could not land until pathways were found and marked across the reef.

The command group of CT8 and BLT 1/8 stayed offshore in landing craft during the night of November 20/21 while awaiting landing orders. That night the expected Japanese counterattack did not happen, likely because US naval gunfire had killed Shibasaki and most of his senior officers. At 0513hrs, November 21, Shoup then ordered BLT 1/8 and CT8's command group to land on Red 2. The first wave reached the reef at 0615hrs and waded 500yd to the beach, suffering heavy casualties in the process. The battalion's progress was helped by the use of 75mm pack howitzers manhandled ashore on D-day. These fired at ranges of 125yd against Japanese positions firing at the wading Marines. Throughout D+1 heavy fighting continued as the Marines expanded their beachhead against fierce resistance.

On D+1, Major Michael P. Ryan, commanding Co. L, 2d Marines, found himself near Betio's western beach with various detachments from his regiment, two M4A2 tanks, and a naval-gunfire spotter in radio contact with the destroyers USS *Ringgold* (DD-500) and USS *Dashiell* (DD-659) off shore. Ryan organized a combined-arms attack to drive to the south side of Betio and secure its western beach (Green Beach). Ryan's attack started at 1120hrs with the two destroyers shelling targets within 50yd of his front. Ryan's force overran the 2d Company, 7th Sasebo SNLF and two 8in, two 140mm, three

Marines hug the ground on Betio as they prepare to move against a Japanese position just beyond the rise in front of them. Most casualties in the first three waves of assault troops occurred after they disembarked from the LVTs that carried them to the beach. The Marine battalions were initially without their supporting heavy weapons. The crew-served weapons were either stranded on conventional landing craft offshore or lost as Marines attempted to carry them ashore while wading across the coral reef. (US Marine Corps)

David M. Shoup

Born December 30, 1904, David Monroe Shoup was commissioned a second lieutenant in the US Marine Corps on July 20, 1926, following graduation from DePauw University, Indiana. His assignments between the world wars included service with the 6th Marines in Tientsin, China, during 1927. In November 1934, he was again sent to China where he served with the 4th Marines in Shanghai and later was stationed at the American Legation in Beijing. A major in May 1941, Shoup went to Iceland with the 6th Marines. While serving in Iceland, he became Operations Officer of the 1st Marine Brigade in October 1941. Promoted to lieutenant colonel in August 1942, he became the 2d Marine Division's Operations and Training Officer. He was responsible for detailed planning of the Tarawa assault. When Colonel William W. Marshall, commander of the 2d Marines (the lead assault regiment), became seriously ill, Shoup was promoted to colonel on November 9, 1943, and given command of the regiment.

On November 20, 1943, Shoup was scheduled to land after the initial waves. After the LVT carrying

him and his advance command team was disabled by enemy fire, Shoup then waded across the coral reef under fire and was wounded by shrapnel in the leg and grazed by a bullet on the neck. When he reached land he immediately started coordinating and organizing aggressive attacks on the Japanese. He remained in command of all troops ashore until late evening November 21, when Colonel Merritt A. Edson, the division's chief of staff, assumed command. Shoup was awarded the Medal of Honor for his actions on Tarawa Atoll.

Shoup continued to serve in the US Marine Corps. In 1949 he was detailed as a technical advisor for the movie Sands of Iwo Jima. Part of the movie's story took place during the assault on Tarawa Atoll and Shoup contributed a cameo performance as himself. Shoup was promoted as the 22d Commandant of the Marine Corps on January 1, 1960, and promoted to the rank of general on the same day. He retired from military service in December 1963 and died in Alexandria, Virginia, on January 13, 1983.

80mm, and two 37mm gun emplacements. At 1225hrs Green Beach was declared secured and Ryan's force turned east and set up defenses. Meanwhile, elements of CT8 attacked eastward from Red Beach along the north shore and part of CT2 attacked south:

> Early afternoon saw the 1st and 2d Battalions, 2d Marines, reach the south coast; the Japanese forces on Betio were now split into two groups. Supplies were getting ashore. Reinforcements were on the way. The picture had brightened perceptibly. Then at 1706, Shoup sent his message to division which ended with these words: * * * Combat efficiency: We are winning. (Stockman 1947: 41)

Once released from Corps reserve, elements of CT6 landed without opposition on Green Beach. According to its commander, Major William K. Jones, BLT 1/6 did so late on November 22, using rubber boats:

> We went in to the beach with an LCVP towing 6 rubber boats and the first wave hit the beach at 1800 – that is, Green Beach South, and the entire battalion was landed by 1835. When the first wave landed, I got the word that Green Beach South was heavily mined, so coming in in a column of companies, I changed the route of approach and landed on the North of Green Beach South. (Quoted in FMFRP 12-90: 53)

Jones deployed his battalion behind Ryan's defense line and prepared a combined-arms attack for November 23. Jones's was the first Marine battalion on Betio in condition to attack as a complete unit.

Shibasaki Keiji

Shibasaki Keiji graduated from the IJN's Naval Academy in 1915. He served on several ships including the heavy cruiser *Chikuma* and the battleship *Yamashiro*. In 1921 he was assigned as navigator on the destroyer *Tachikaze* and in 1936, became commander of the gunboat *Ataka*. Shibasaki was promoted to captain in 1937 and served on several staffs, including a year as chief of staff to the Shanghai SNLF. In all, he spent 19 months as an officer with the SNLF in China. While commanding the Kure local defense squadron, Shibasaki was promoted to rear admiral on May 1, 1943. He arrived at Tarawa Atoll in September 1943 and assumed command of the 3d SBF.

Until his assignment to command the 3d SBF, Shibasaki's career was unremarkable. He had experience of Japanese amphibious landings against the Chinese and understood many of the problems inherent to these operations. He did not have combat experience

against Americans, however, and had not encountered their greater firepower and new technologies. He concentrated the Japanese defensive efforts on Betio Island toward destroying any attacker at the shoreline; failing that his men would promptly counterattack and destroy any enemy lodgment. Shibasaki worked hard to train his men and keep their morale high. He is alleged to have claimed that the Americans could not capture Tarawa Atoll in 100 years with 1 million men. If he did say this, it was hyperbole to inspire his troops.

After the fighting for Tarawa Atoll the United States assumed Shibasaki had been killed in the battle or had committed suicide once defeat was obvious. A postwar report (cited in Alexander 1995) asserts that he, along with his senior staff, was killed by naval gunfire while trying to move to a different command post on D-day. After the battle, Shibasaki was posthumously promoted to vice admiral.

During the night of November 22/23, Colonel Merritt A. Edson, the divisional chief of staff, took command on Betio. Edson's subordinates were Shoup (CT2) and Colonel Elmer E. Hall (CT8). BLT 1/6 was attached to CT2. The plan for D+2 was for BLT 1/8 to eliminate Japanese positions between Red 1 and Red 2; the rest of CT8 was to attack eastward on the lagoon side, and BLT 1/6 was to attack eastward and link up with troops of CT2 on the south shore 400yd east of the airstrip's western end. US Navy ships would shell Betio east of the airstrip's turning circle (on the east end of the airstrip). Battleships would use their main batteries no closer than 500yd from Marines' lines. Within 500yd, 5in naval gunfire would be employed. The US shelling plan called for a 20-minute barrage at 0700hrs, another at 0830hrs, a third at 0930hrs, and a fourth at 1030hrs. By daybreak D+2, five 75mm pack howitzer batteries were ready to fire – two on nearby Bairiki Island and three on Betio near Red Beach – and a sixth battery (on Bairiki) was ready at noon.

BLT 1/6 planned its attack for 0800hrs with one M4A2 medium tank and seven M3A1 light tanks. One M3A1 stayed with the battalion headquarters to provide a radio link with the other tanks. The front was constrained to 100yd between the south edge of the airstrip and Betio's south shore. The battalion deployed in a column of companies with Co. C in the lead, then Co. B, and Co. A in the rear. With such a narrow front, Co. C attacked with one platoon. A heavy-machine-gun platoon was attached to each rifle company. An attached platoon of combat engineers and two flamethrowers were assigned to Co. C. With a fresh and intact battalion supported by tanks, artillery, and naval gunfire, this attack was primed for success.

Delayed five minutes, Co. C started its advance at 0805hrs. It soon became necessary to expand to a two-platoon front to provide enough infantry to oppose the large number of Japanese defensive positions encountered.

The light tanks moved forward, staying within 10–15yd of their following Marines who prevented Japanese from attacking the tanks with magnetic mines. The 37mm main gun on the M3A1 light tanks could not destroy the ruggedly constructed Japanese positions, so the tanks would suppress a Japanese position by shelling and machine-gunning it. Once it was suppressed, infantry and combat engineers would approach and reduce the position with demolition charges or flamethrowers.

On the northern end of the battalion's front, the M4A2 medium tank moved along the airstrip to avoid Japanese suicide attackers. The tank's 75mm main gun proved far more effective in destroying Japanese fortifications. Once, when a 75mm round penetrated a coconut-log fighting position, the occupants swarmed out and attacked the tank. Accompanying Marine infantry promptly engaged the Japanese with rifles and BARs while the M4A2 maneuvered in circles, crushing some of the enemy and providing the Marines with clear fields of fire.

BLT 1/6 advanced 900yd, clearing the coastal defense positions along the southern beach. Resistance was initially light, but increased as the battalion advanced. Japanese defenses on the south shore were built facing seaward and proved vulnerable to attack from the flank and rear. Naval-gunfire support, divisional artillery, and infantry/tank cooperation proved effective in eliminating Japanese defenses and reducing Marine casualties; about 250 Japanese were killed by the battalion during its advance. Visual contact with the battered CT2 on the south shore was gained at 1015hrs and physical contact was made around 1100hrs.

Before making contact with CT2, Jones was ordered to report to Shoup's command post to attend the afternoon attack planning meeting. Except for a pocket of Japanese defenders stubbornly holding out against BLT 3/2 and BLT 1/8 between Red 1 and Red 2, the western portion of Betio was secured.

Red Beach on D-day as men of either the 2d or 8th Marines shelter behind the coconut-log barricade on Betio while awaiting orders to advance and expand the beachhead. The men are on the lagoon side of the barricade that had been built by the Japanese. In the background a half-sunk LVT is visible. To the right, the barrel of a .30-caliber light machine gun is visible and ammunition belts are near the foreground. Some of these Marines may be members of a light-machine-gun team. (US Marine Corps)

The afternoon attack would be made by BLT 1/6 in conjunction with the now-depleted BLT 2/8 and BLT 3/8, both of which would clear the enemy from around the eastern turning circle of the airstrip and the lagoon shore. Jones's BLT 1/6 would make the main effort, attacking eastward toward the end of the airstrip. The battalion was supported by tanks, two battalions of 75mm howitzers of the 10th Marines, and naval gunfire. After linking up with CT2, BLT 1/6 had reorganized and placed Co. A in the lead. The tropical heat caused many cases of heat prostration during the morning. With water supplies low, only a small portion of Co. A could replenish its water supply before attacking.

Co. A and the light tanks attacked at 1330hrs. Some 75yd behind Co. A was Co. B, followed by Co. C in reserve. Immediately, Co. A came under fire from well-organized Japanese positions. Part of the fire came from a turret-type emplacement near the beach, but the light tanks could not destroy or neutralize this position with their 37mm main guns. This one Japanese position stopped the Marines' attack for nearly 90 minutes until a medium tank was brought up and neutralized it with 75mm gunfire. Jones reported:

> Shortly after 1300 we ran into heavy enemy resistance and made about 300 to 400 yards that afternoon. About 1500 I was ordered to relieve [Major Henry P.] Crowe's battalion on my left with a company, and "C" company was assigned to that mission. From 1545 on I had no contact with that company because their TBY [radio] went out of commission. With the assignment of "C" Company to relieve the CT8 battalion, all my companies were committed. "A" Company had been passed through "B" Company, which had so much trouble that "A" moved around them. "A" Company's left flank was touching the air strip. About 1830 all tanks were recalled. Companies "A" and "B" were ordered to consolidate their positions and await orders, and were held there for the night. Companies "A" and

Rear Admiral Shibasaki's command post on Betio was this large reinforced-concrete structure, depicted here after the fighting had ended. It was hit multiple times during the bombardment but was not destroyed. After the war, an SNLF survivor reported that on D-day, for reasons that are unclear, Shibasaki attempted to move to an alternative command-post position. While outside the concrete structure, a naval shell landed in his immediate vicinity, killing him and his senior staff. The damaged Type 95 Ha-Gō light tank in front of the building may have been intended to convey him to this alternative command post. (US Marine Corps)

"B", particularly the latter, lost many men, mostly by machine guns. (Quoted in FMFRP 12-90: 53)

Co. A was in visual contact across the airstrip's turning circle with Co. C. BLT 1/6 organized positions for the night and covered the open ground between Co. A and Co. C with .30-caliber medium machine guns. As night approached, Jones's battalion prepared for an expected Japanese charge:

... If the Japanese ever intended to launch a counterattack, this was the night to do it. Each night the Marines had dug in with the uneasy feeling that before morning the Japanese would stage a "banzai." So far, the mad, suicidal, headlong rush had not come. Jones made every preparation to repel such an attack when his companies organized their positions at dusk on 22 November. (Stockman 1947: 51)

Around 1930hrs, some 50 Japanese counterattacked BLT 1/6's lines. Infiltrating between outposts, they found a small gap between Co. A and Co. B. With all three of his rifle companies in the front lines, Jones's reserve was made up of his 81mm mortar platoon and men from his headquarters and weapons companies. He committed this force, which eliminated the infiltrators and restored the battalion's lines by 2030hrs. The battalion exercised excellent effective fire discipline, preventing the Japanese attackers from locating its automatic weapons. Marines relied on bayonets and hand grenades to repel the enemy while artillery fire was brought as close as 75yd to the forward US fighting positions. Expecting another attack, Jones requested US Navy destroyers to shell the eastern end of Betio from 500yd east of his lines to the extreme eastern tip of the island. Between his front lines and the destroyers' fire zone, the 10th Marines placed near-continuous harassment

Owing to the shortage of LVTs, many of the Marines who landed on Betio after the first three waves had to wade ashore for up to 500yd over the coral reef. Many wading Marines were shot by the Japanese as they tried to reach the shore. Some units suffered heavy casualties and several battalions reached the shore disorganized and without many of their heavy weapons. Given the orderly appearance of the Marines in this photograph, these may be men of the 6th Marines landing late on D+1 after Green Beach, the western end of Betio, had been secured. (US Marine Corps)

shelling. These 75mm howitzers would shift from harassment to defensive barrages when the Japanese attacked.

A second Japanese counterattack began at 2300hrs. One group drew the attention of Co. A by firing small arms, throwing hand grenades, yelling, and moving around. Another group attacked Co. B, which repelled it with machine guns, 60mm mortars, and hand grenades. This fighting appears to have caused the Japanese to think Co. B's position was weak because they launched their final, and heaviest, counterattack there. Around 0300hrs, November 23, Japanese troops started firing heavy and light machine guns at BLT 1/6's lines from gun positions located in wrecked trucks just 50yd from the Marines. Several of these positions were put out of action by heavy-machine-gun fire. Three of the Japanese positions were destroyed by Marines who crawled forward and threw hand grenades into them.

At 0400hrs, November 23, about 300 Japanese troops charged all along Co. B's front and along the right of Co. A. The left front of Co. A was targeted by a loud diversionary party. Artillery fire from the 10th Marines was called in to within 75yd of the front lines and US Navy destroyers bombarded the eastern end of Betio. By 0500hrs the attack had ended; the bodies of over 200 Japanese dead were left within 50yd of BLT 1/6's front lines. Within the area shelled by the 10th Marines were another 125 bodies.

At 0800hrs, November 23, the fresh BLT 3/6 attacked through BLT 1/6's lines. By 1310hrs these Marines reached the eastern tip of Betio, killing 475 Japanese and capturing 14 in the process. Lieutenant Colonel Kenneth F. McLeod, commander of BLT 3/6, reported: "At no time was there any determined defensive. I did not use artillery at all and called for naval gunfire for only about five minutes, which was all the support used by me. We used flamethrowers and could have used more. Medium tanks were excellent. My light tanks didn't fire a shot" (quoted in FMFRP 12-90: 57).

Marines attacking to expand the beachhead on D-day. Betio had little elevation; this modest sand hill was one of the few elevated features. Marines used these sand hills for cover when possible just as the Japanese used them for defensive positions. Unlike larger islands where artillery observers used elevated ground for observation posts, on atolls the few elevated features became targets for air strikes and naval shelling. (US Marine Corps)

Namur Island, Kwajalein Atoll

February 1–2, 1944

BACKGROUND TO BATTLE

In early December 1943 Admiral Chester W. Nimitz, Commander-in-Chief Pacific Fleet and Commander-in-Chief Pacific Ocean Area, decided to accelerate the Marshalls attack codenamed Operation *Flintlock*. Instead of capturing one of four heavily defended eastern atolls – Wotje, Maloelap, Mille, or Jaluit – he decided to capture Kwajalein Atoll and bypass the other four. Undefended Majuro Atoll was added to serve as an advanced fleet base. D-day was set for January 31, 1944. Kwajalein Atoll contained two major objectives: Kwajalein Island (the atoll's southeast corner) and the twin islands of Roi-Namur (the atoll's northern tip).

The Japanese expected an attack on the eastern Marshalls first and concentrated on building up the defenses of Wotje, Maloelap, Mille, and Jaluit:

> Just as he had startled his subordinates by proposing an immediate attack on Kwajalein, Nimitz also surprised his adversaries. "There was divided opinion as to whether you would land at Jaluit or Mille," a Japanese naval officer confessed after the war. "Some thought you would land on Wotje, but there were few who thought you would go right to the heart of the Marshalls and take Kwajalein." (Shaw, Nalty, & Turnbladh 1966: 139)

Roi and Namur were the 4th Marine Division's main objectives. Their defenses were weak compared to those on Tarawa Atoll. A postwar Japanese report (SDB 1951: 32) estimated that Roi-Namur was defended by 2,920 men. Of these 1,900 were IJN personnel: 400 men of the 61st Naval Guard Unit and 1,500 stranded naval-aviation personnel formed into the Yamada Detachment. The rest were civilians of the 4th Fleet Construction Department, the Naval Air Depot, and the Naval Stores Department. Between 150 and 200 civilians were conscripted Korean laborers. Each island had a battery of two twin-mount 127mm dual-purpose guns; on Namur the guns were located near the northern tip.

Namur also had five 20mm dual-purpose machine cannons, one 37mm rapid-fire gun, six 13mm machine guns, and ten pillboxes each with a 7.7mm machine gun. The beaches were lined with trenches and rifle pits. Inland, Namur's north-central area included a maze of trenches located in heavy undergrowth. Namur was covered in palm trees and the Japanese had built numerous concrete buildings to serve as offices, workshops, warehouses, and magazines. There were no heavy underground defenses on either island. The lagoon shores of both were lightly defended with no underwater or beach obstacles. In accordance with their doctrine, Japanese commanders ordered their men to destroy an enemy landing force on the beaches and to promptly counterattack any lodgment established.

Operation *Flintlock*'s D-day was set for January 31, 1944, when Majuro Atoll was bloodlessly captured by US forces and several small islands of Kwajalein Atoll around Roi-Namur and Kwajalein Island were seized to open passages into the lagoon and provide locations to emplace field artillery to support the main landings. Throughout D-day, US Navy ships pounded the main objectives to soften them up. Based on lessons learned from the fighting on Tarawa Atoll, battleships, cruisers, and destroyers moved in close to the coral-reef edges and used ammunition selected for best effect against specific targets. After the day's bombardment, destroyers kept up harassing fires during the night.

Roi and Namur were invaded on February 1, 1944. Capturing Roi was RCT23's mission while the capture of Namur was assigned to RCT24. The composition of RCT23 was built around the reinforced 23d Marines whereas RCT24 was composed of the 24th Marines plus the following: the 2d Composite Battalion, 20th Marines (one company each of combat engineers, pioneers, and Seabees); Co. B, 4th Tank Battalion (light tanks); 10th Amphibian Tractor Battalion; Cos. B and D, 1st Armored Amphibian Battalion; elements of 4th Special Weapons Battalion; and medical, transport, and communications detachments.

A new type of unit made its debut in the Marshalls fighting; Joint Assault Signal Companies (JASCOs). The Marine 1st JASCO was activated in October 1943 and assigned to the 4th Marine Division for Operation *Flintlock*. A JASCO was organized into shore- and beach-party communications teams, air-liaison parties, and shore fire-control parties. Each assault regiment had a regimental naval-gunfire liaison section consisting of one naval officer and five enlisted men. Each assault battalion was assigned a shore fire-support party consisting of a naval-gunfire liaison section (with one naval officer and seven enlisted Marines) and a forward observer's section (with one Marine officer and seven enlisted Marines). The communications channels were structured so that

Support ships were in direct communication with their assigned party and with the Force Commander via the naval gunfire support common channel. In other words, all fire support ships and all shore fire control parties, as well as regimental naval gunfire liaison officers, were all in instant communication with each other on the naval gunfire support common channel. The details of conducting fires were handled on separate circuits between the individual shore fire control party and its assigned fire support ship. (COMINCH 1944b: 3-13)

MAP KEY

1 1155hrs, February 1: 43 minutes after RCT24 is ordered to proceed across the line of departure, BLT 3/24 lands on Green 1; Cos. I and K drive toward the O-1 line while remaining organized in the assault and boat teams used to load the LVTs.

2 1155hrs, February 1: Co. F, BLT 2/24 lands on the right of Green 2.

3 1200hrs, February 1: Co. E, BLT 2/24 lands in the middle of Green 2 with its right-flank platoon behind Co. F.

4 1210hrs, February 1: Half of Co. G, BLT 2/24, lands on Green 2.

5 1240hrs, February 1: Co. B, BLT 1/24 lands on Green 1 using LCVPs and is attached to BLT 3/24.

6 1300hrs, February 1: Cos. E and F reach the O-1 line, but stop due to enemy fire and to reorganize from boat teams into their normal units.

7 1305hrs, February 1: A massive explosion occurs when a Japanese aerial torpedo storage bunker, mistaken for a pillbox, is attacked by a demolition team. BLT 2/24 loses 20 killed and 100 wounded.

8 1330hrs, February 1: The remainder of Co. G lands on Green 2.

9 1630hrs, February 1: BLT 3/24 and Co. B attack northward from the O-1 line.

10 1640hrs, February 1: Co. K is sent to secure the sand spit between Namur and neighboring Roi.

11 1830hrs, February 1: Co. I and supporting tanks attack along the west shore, but are recalled because they lack support to their east.

12 1930hrs, February 1: All US units are ordered to dig in for the night.

13 0630hrs, February 2: Japanese troops attack Co. I. US medium tanks are brought up and repel the attack.

14 0900hrs, February 2: BLT 3/24 attacks toward the north shore and Natalie Point.

15 1005hrs, February 2: BLT 1/24 and BLT 2/24 are combined and attack toward Natalie Point.

16 1100hrs, February 2: BLT 3/24 reaches the site of a wrecked 127mm dual-purpose gun battery near Natalie Point and encounters heavy resistance from Japanese infantry.

17 1215hrs, February 2: BLT 3/24 overcomes resistance and advances to Natalie Point, meeting BLT 1/24.

18 1418hrs, February 2: The 4th Marine Division declares Namur secured.

Battlefield environment

Kwajalein Atoll is at 8°43′N, 167°44′E and has a lagoon covering 839 square miles. Namur Island, the location of the featured action, is in the northern part of the lagoon. In February 1944, the greatest distance between the lagoon beaches and the north shore was about 750yd; from east to west it was about 950yd. The highest natural elevation was less than 10ft. The island was covered with a heavy growth of palm trees wherever construction had not taken place. Heavy bombing and shelling wrecked the trees, shattering many and knocking others down. Soil quality was poor and the island's surface was rocky and rough, similar to that of Betio Island. The Japanese had built a number of concrete buildings for use as offices and workshops, but these were not designed as fortifications. Many of the buildings, not having been designed for defense, were damaged.

Namur's climate is equatorial, meaning it is hot and humid. February's average high temperature is 86.5°F and the relative humidity is 76.1 percent. These combine to give a heat index

of 99°F. As on Tarawa Atoll, men required large amounts of drinking water to stay hydrated. Water had to be brought ashore from ships to replenish Marines' canteens during the battle.

Without an airfield, Namur had been built up by the Japanese so as to resemble a small town. They built a pier extending across the reef into the lagoon for unloading ships bringing men and materiel to the island. Americans named this the Yokohama Pier, and it connected to a network of roads which ran around and across the island, creating a layout analogous to city blocks in the southern and central part of the island. Palm trees were left standing around many buildings and over most of the island's northern part. The trees provided some degree of cover from aerial reconnaissance, until the pre-invasion bombardment shattered or knocked down many of them. Namur had more potential infantry defense positions than Roi. Buildings and dense shattered vegetation forced attacking Marines to move cautiously; and had to be cleared of defenders as if the fighting was in a town.

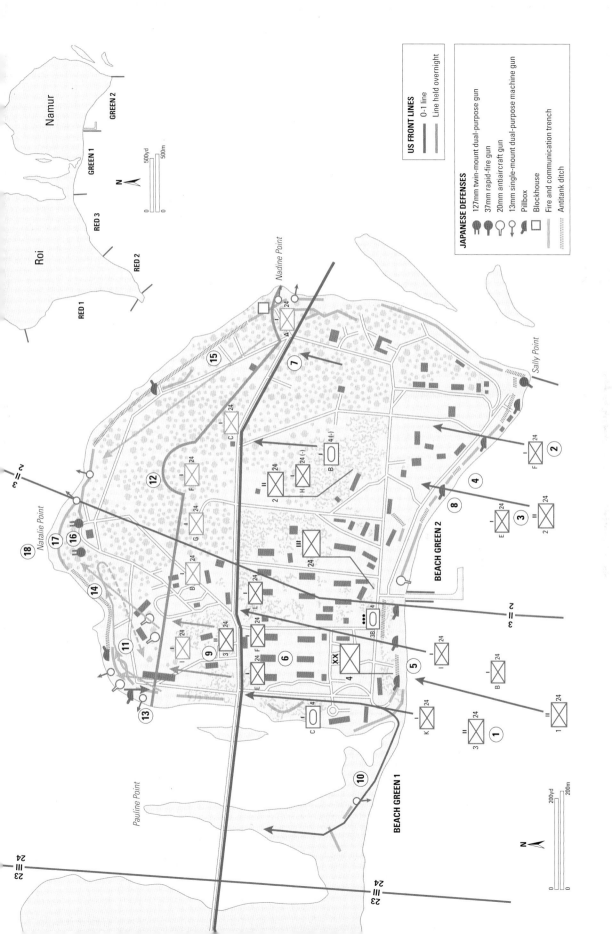

Namur

Roi

GREEN 2

GREEN 1

RED 3

RED 2

RED 1

N

500yd
500m

Nadine Point

Sally Point

BEACH GREEN 2

Natalie Point

Pauline Point

BEACH GREEN 1

N

200yd
200m

US FRONT LINES

0–1 line

Line held overnight

JAPANESE DEFENSES

127mm twin-mount dual-purpose gun

37mm rapid-fire gun

20mm antiaircraft gun

13mm single-mount dual-purpose machine gun

Pillbox

Blockhouse

Fire and communication trench

Antitank ditch

INTO COMBAT

On February 1, Roi Island was captured by RCT23 in just six hours and 32 minutes – the first LVT(A) ("A" for Armored) landing was at 1133hrs and the island was declared secured at 1805hrs: "Supporting weapons, especially naval gunfire, had done their work so well that the Japanese were incapable of putting up a coordinated defense. The level terrain enabled Marine tanks to roam the island at will. The fight for Roi had been an easy one. Such was not the case on neighboring Namur" (Shaw, Nalty, & Turnbladh 1966: 167). One reason for Roi's smooth capture was that RCT23 had its full allotment of 110 operational LVTs. In contrast, Colonel Franklin A. Hart's RCT24 had only 62 LVTs operable of the 110 allotted after their heavy use on January 31.

Japanese defenses on Namur's lagoon-side beaches consisted of infantry fire trenches and antitank ditches, six pillboxes mounting 7.7mm machine guns, one 20mm dual-purpose automatic cannon, and one 37mm rapid-fire cannon. The assault was made by two BLTs of RCT24: BLT 2/24 (Lieutenant Colonel Francis H. Brink) and BLT 3/24 (Lieutenant Colonel Austin R. Brunelli). BLT 1/24 (Lieutenant Colonel Aquilla J. Dyess) was in reserve. Beaches were designated from west to east as Green 1 (BLT 3/24) and Green 2 (BLT 2/24). Each BLT was to land on a two-company front: Cos. E and F for BLT 2/24

The north shore of Namur photographed from a US Navy observation aircraft during the pre-landing bombardment. The area covered by palm trees is visible through the rising smoke. Roads, trails, and buildings are identifiable. To the right, a coastal defense gun position is visible just behind the ocean beach. The vulnerability of Japanese atoll defenses, once air superiority was held by the US Navy, is apparent. (US Navy)

and Cos. I and K for BLT 3/24. Each BLT kept its third company (Co. G for BLT 2/24 and Co. L for BLT 3/24) in reserve.

US naval-gunfire preparation began at 0650hrs, February 1, with two battleships, one heavy cruiser, one light cruiser, and two destroyers. Also firing in support were 1st and 2nd battalions, 14th Marines, with 75mm pack howitzers on nearby islands. On Ennugarret Island, 400yd southeast of Namur and captured the day before, five self-propelled 75mm guns, 17 37mm antitank guns, nine 60mm mortars, four 81mm mortars, and 61 machine guns provided fire support to the right flank of BLT 2/24. The effect of air and naval bombardment was summarized in a postwar Japanese report: "Due to the aerial and naval bombardment ... the island literally changed its shape. Because of the incompleteness of defensive positions a great number of the garrison force were killed or injured. By the time the enemy landed, the great majority of our men were dead or wounded" (SDB 1951).

Hart's landing plan was disrupted from the start by the shortage of LVTs, according to the commanding general of the 4th Marine Division, Major General Harry Schmidt: "The major difficulty [at Namur] was, of course, the inability of the amtrac crews to meet H-Hour on the morning of the principal assault ... Many of them could not find their parent ships and many needed service and gas. Many Navy transport commanders were to blame in not providing help at this time" (quoted in Heinl & Crown 1952: 82).

Landing time (W-hour) was delayed from 1000hrs to 1100hrs. Although each rifle company in the two assault battalions was intended to have 12 LVTs, in BLT 2/24, Co. G had only three and Co. F seven, while Co. E in reserve had its allocated 12; Cos. E and G therefore switched roles. Co. F was without elements of its 2d, 3rd, and Weapons platoons, so these were placed in two LCVPs and accompanied the LVTs. Co. G was finally loaded into seven LVTs and two LCVPs. BLT 3/24 had similar LVT issues. Brunelli redistributed his available LVTs so each assault company had 12, but this left Co. L without any landing craft and the battalion with no ready reserve.

An aerial photograph of the lagoon off Namur during the invasion. LVTs can be seen leaving the island and heading back to ships in the transport area to embark more Marines. In the foreground another wave of landing craft heads toward the beach. Smoke from the air and naval bombardment rises from Namur. Also visible are the coral reefs surrounding the island and the lagoon. (US Navy)

Movement toward the beach began at 1112hrs, but RCT24 was not ready. However, when the control destroyer USS *Phelps* (DD-360) signaled the waves to proceed, Hart decided his RCT would attack as it was. The US Marine Corps' Official History states: "Both Brink's 2/24 and Brunelli's 3/24 had difficulty in getting enough tractors for their commands, and some last-minute arrivals were being fitted into the formation when the destroyer *Phelps* signaled the LVTs to start shore-ward. The firepower of supporting weapons helped compensate for the lack of organization" (Shaw, Nalty, & Turnbladh 1966: 167). With BLT 3/24's reserve company unavailable, Hart ordered Co. B of BLT 1/24 to join BLT 3/24. BLT 1/24 was the RCT reserve embarked in LCVPs. Fortunately, there was adequate water over the coral reef for the LCVPs.

Supporting firepower included LVT(A)s of Cos. B and D, 1st Armored Amphibian Battalion, and six LCI(G)s – Landing Craft Infantry (Gun). As the landing force proceeded toward the beach, the US air, naval, and artillery bombardment intensified. Once the first wave of LVTs was 750yd off the beach, air bombardment ceased; when 500yd out, the ships lifted fire. After a two-minute pause the ships resumed shelling targets beyond the first objective line (O-1 line), approximately 300yd north of the lagoon. LCI(G)s moved along the flanks of the landing craft; 1,000yd from the beach the LCI(G)s fired 4.5in rocket barrages onto the beaches then moved closer and used their 40mm and 20mm cannons plus .50-caliber heavy machine guns to engage and suppress enemy positions. LVT(A)s preceded the LVTs carrying troops; these were to advance 100yd inland, but antitank ditches, debris, and a maze of trenches and craters prevented the LVT(A)s from doing so. As Marine riflemen dismounted and advanced, the stopped LVT(A)s provided fire support with their 37mm guns and .30-caliber machine guns until masked by the infantry.

At 1155hrs, BLT 3/24 began landing on Green 1. Within minutes the two assault companies, Cos. I and K, began to advance toward the O-1 line. The US Marine Corps' *esprit de corps* and training shone as the problem of intermixed units on the beach was instantly solved: "the major part of one platoon from Company I landed in the K/24 zone and approximately the same number from K in the I/24 zone. These units advanced directly inland, remaining with their 'adopted' companies until the O–1 Line was gained" (Shaw, Nalty, & Turnbladh 1966: 170).

The Marines moved to the attack as soon as they debarked from their LVTs. Brunelli recalled: "Each boat team attacked straight to its front, under the leadership of its boat team commander, until reaching the initial objective O-1" (quoted in Heinl & Crown 1952: 88). Assault companies' platoons were each divided into an assault team and two boat teams. The assault team, led by the platoon commander, was organized to reduce pillboxes, blockhouses, and other fortifications. It contained a demolitions group, a bazooka group, a light-machine-gun group, and a support group. The two boat teams, under senior NCOs, consisted of the rest of the platoon. Each boat team was trained to fight as a unit until the platoon's normal organization was reestablished once ashore. The 4th Marine Division ordered assault companies to fight using these teams until the O-1 line had been secured. This kept the assault's momentum going and denied the Japanese defenders time to recover and reorganize.

KWAJALEIN · USMC PHOTO · NO. K-3

Marine riflemen and combat engineers worked together to destroy pillboxes, bunkers, and covered emplacements. Small groups of Japanese, mostly aviation and construction personnel, fought to the death in shattered positions and trenches. Other small groups of defenders hid in rubble and vegetation and were dealt with by advancing reserve units. With Japanese communications lines cut, their island command post destroyed, and senior leaders killed by the preparatory bombardment, each small group of defenders fought alone.

By 1240hrs, Co. B of BLT 1/24 had landed on Green 1 and moved inland, eliminating bypassed defenders as and when they were encountered. Also landed were two 75mm self-propelled mounts (SPMs), shore party, and other support elements of BLT 2/24. One 75mm SPM joined the advancing Marines, while the second suffered a drowned engine. Around 1300hrs, three light tanks from the 4th Tank Battalion landed on Green 1 and moved forward. By 1400hrs BLT 1/24 had reached the O-1 line and paused. Cos. I and K reorganized from their boat-team structure back into normal platoon and company organizations. Co. L, stranded on its LST because of the lack of LVTs, finally landed by LCVPs at 1530hrs. While paused, BLT 1/24 prepared for a coordinated regimental attack scheduled for 1630hrs.

Meanwhile, Co. F of BLT 2/24 landed on the right side of Green 2 at 1155hrs, followed five minutes later by Co. E – but instead of landing

Marines on one of Roi-Namur's beaches shelter from Japanese fire. In the distance, smoke from the pre-assault naval-gunfire barrage is rising. By this point in the ship-to-shore movement, naval gunfire has shifted to targets beyond the immediate beach. Naval-gunfire missions close to the Marines were under the control of specialized Navy–Marine fire-control parties and were fired against specific targets. (US Marine Corps)

on the left side of the beach, Co. E landed in the middle, which meant some of it was behind Co. F and some to the left. A large antitank ditch then prevented the LVTs from moving 100yd inland as planned. Forced to dismount from their LVTs, both companies immediately advanced inland remaining in their assault- and boat-team organizations. They pushed on toward the O-1 line, roughly 300–450yd from the beach. Each platoon was led by its assault team, followed by its two boat teams that mopped up bypassed defenders. Thick vegetation, in places as high as 6ft, reduced visibility to a few feet. Combined with Co. E having landed to the right of its intended zone, a gap developed between the left flank of the advance and the boundary with BLT 3/24.

At 1210hrs, about half of Co. G landed on Green 2, the rest landing around 1330hrs. BLT 2/24's headquarters landed at 1215hrs and Brink assumed command. He sent part of Co. G to clear the left flank and reach the boundary line with BLT 3/24. They advanced 175yd easily before being stopped by defenders dug into a thicket. By 1300hrs they were stopped by enemy fire from the front and flanks. At the same time, Cos. E and F reached the O-1 line and stopped to reorganize and untangle their mixed troops.

At 1305hrs, an assault team from Co. F was trying to reduce what was thought to be a Japanese pillbox. After blowing a hole in its side with a shaped charge, the Marines hurled satchel charges into the structure. Unfortunately, this was an aerial torpedo warhead storage bunker and a massive explosion occurred. Shortly after, the Japanese apparently detonated two smaller

Marines cautiously move forward through the remains of trees and buildings on Namur Island as they try to locate and eliminate Japanese resistance. Though damaged, concrete structures and rubble provided infantry with ad hoc fighting positions. (US Marine Corps)

ammunition storage bunkers nearby. These explosions killed 20 and wounded 100 of BLT 2/24's men – 50 percent of RCT24's casualties on Namur. Among the wounded was Brink, who remained in command of his battalion. The explosions knocked out most of BLT 2/24's communications and forced reliance on message runners. Hart attached Co. A to BLT 2/24 to offset the losses caused by the explosions.

At 1630hrs, BLT 3/24 plus Co. B attacked northward from the O-1 line. Because of the delay in doing so, "the Japanese had shaken off some of the dazing effects of the bombardment. There was still no organized resistance in the usual sense, but pockets of defenders poured forth machine-gun and rifle fire, backed up by mortars and rifle grenades. The debris and damaged buildings, as well as the dense jungle growth, made the going all the more difficult" (Heinl & Crown 1952: 93). Cos. I and B led the attack, Co. L was in reserve, and Co. K was sent to secure the sand spit between Roi and Namur. Light tanks and LVT(A)s fired on bunkers and pinned down the Japanese so that Marines could place demolition charges against the bunkers. The light tanks in turn needed the infantry to provide protection from the Japanese defenders, who would swarm an unescorted tank and attack it with hand grenades and demolition charges.

BLT 2/24 had been reinforced with Co. A at 1530hrs and Co. C at 1600hrs. From left to right, BLT 2/24 now had the following companies in its front line: half of Co. G (the other half was in the rear), Co. F, Co. C (with elements of Co. E attached), and Co. A. At 1730hrs, BLT 2/24 attacked.

The great explosion on Namur as viewed from a US Navy aircraft shortly after it happened. This was caused when demolition charges were thrown into a concrete structure thought to be a defensive position. Instead, it was an aerial torpedo storage bunker. This large explosion accounted for about half of all the 2/24th Marines' losses in the fighting on Namur. (US Navy)

On its left, light tanks of Co. B, 4th Tank Battalion, supported the advance. These Marines advanced to within 35yd of the north shore. Because their flanks were uncovered, however, they were pulled back. On the US right, the advance was able to only move a short distance beyond the O-1 line.

Around 1800hrs, the 4th Marine Division's headquarters landed on Namur and assumed command of the Marines on Roi and Namur. The division quickly ordered RCT23's reserve (3d Battalion) and M4A2 medium tanks to cross from Roi to Namur and reinforce RCT24. The 3d Battalion was not used, however, and remained in reserve. One platoon of M4A2s was assigned to BLT 3/24 at 1830hrs and, with one 75mm SPM and elements of Co. I, attacked northward along the west shore. This small team reached a position near the northern tip of Namur, but was pulled back because it was unsupported on both flanks. All US units were ordered to dig in for the night at 1930hrs and prepare to resist possible nighttime Japanese counterattacks. With their command fragmented and lacking communications, the Japanese continued to fight as scattered uncoordinated groups. A Japanese counterattack was made at dawn against Co. I in approximately company strength. Four medium tanks soon reinforced the Marines and in 35 minutes the counterattack was over.

Hart set 0900hrs as the time for his regiment to attack and complete the capture of Namur. On the left flank, BLT 3/24 had in line (west to east) Cos. K, I, and L, with Co. B in reserve. These were supported by two platoons

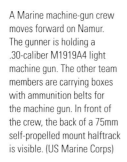

A Marine machine-gun crew moves forward on Namur. The gunner is holding a .30-caliber M1919A4 light machine gun. The other team members are carrying boxes with ammunition belts for the machine gun. In front of the crew, the back of a 75mm self-propelled mount halftrack is visible. (US Marine Corps)

KWAJALEIN   U.S.M.C. PHOTO   NO. K-4

of M4A2s. BLT 2/24's front line (west to east) consisted of Cos. G, F, C, and A, with Co. E in reserve. Because Brink had been wounded on February 1 (during the aerial torpedo storage bunker explosion), Dyess, commander of BLT 1/24, took charge of this force, which now included two of his battalion's three rifle companies. Supporting the combined BLTs 1/24 and 2/24 were one platoon of M4A2s, light tanks of Co. B, 4th Tank Battalion, and several 75mm SPMs. Both battalions were to mop up any Japanese defenders as they advanced.

BLT 3/24 attacked at 0900hrs. The Marines encountered steady and desperate resistance from Japanese within thick foliage, concrete buildings, rubble, and remaining pillboxes. With the support of M4A2s, BLT 3/24 was able to reduce Japanese positions with relatively low casualties. The M4A2s fired 75mm armor-piercing rounds to crack the concrete of the pillboxes and then fired high-explosive rounds at the cracks to open holes in each structure. By 1100hrs, BLT 3/24 closed with the Japanese defenders positioned around the damaged 127mm gun battery near the northern point of Namur. Supported by tanks, Co. L eliminated this center of resistance and reached the shore at 1215hrs. Few Japanese surrendered; most chose to die fighting or to commit suicide.

The attack of the combined BLTs 1/24 and 2/24 was delayed until 1005hrs as they had to wait for their assigned M4A2s. The team's left flank had to destroy a blockhouse with the support of the M4A2s and 75mm

Men of the 4th Marine Division fire on Japanese positions on the twin islands of Roi-Namur. These Marines are using the concrete foundation of a metal building as an improvised fighting position. In the distance is a mix of shattered and standing palm trees. In the foreground are pieces of twisted sheet metal from the destroyed building. (US Marine Corps)

Namur Island, February 2, 1944

Between 1100hrs and 1200hrs, an infantry/tank team from Co. I, 3d Battalion, 24th Marines, and M4A2 medium tanks from Co. C (Medium), 4th Tank Battalion, reached the location toward one of the two twin 127mm dual-purpose gun mounts near the north shore of Namur Island. These guns had been disabled during the pre-invasion air and naval bombardment. The vegetation was thick and tangled even after the intense bombardment, but some palm trees were still standing. To the right is a concrete building, one built by the Japanese to house supplies and provide offices. This building was not designed as a fortification and had been damaged, as was the 127mm gun mount, during the pre-invasion bombardment.

In front of the 127mm gun mount, IJN sailors are firing on the advancing Marines. The defenders include men of the 61st Naval Guard Unit and improvised infantry of the Yamada Detachment. The latter was formed weeks before the US attack from aviation ground units of the IJN's 24th Air Flotilla along with naval supply and administration personnel. These sailors received rudimentary ground-combat training and were equipped with infantry small arms, light machine guns, and a small number of grenade dischargers.

The Marines provided protection to the M4A2 medium tank while it in turn supported the Marines with its 75mm main gun. Close infantry/tank teamwork was critical. If a tank did not have infantry support with it, Japanese troops would attack it with hand grenades, demolition charges, and when available, magnetic antitank mines. Japanese troops would even crawl under a tank to attach an antitank mine. The M4A2 used its machine guns to suppress Japanese troops in trenches and foxholes, permitting Marines to close and eliminate resistance. Additionally, its 75mm main gun could blast holes in pillboxes and bunkers, destroying these or enabling engineers to place demolition charges to complete their reduction.

Fighting on Namur, and the other islands of Kwajalein Atoll, was a preview of future combat in the Pacific Theater of Operations. As the US advance moved westward, more IJA and IJN rear-area units were converted to improvised infantry. Defeating these units cost many American lives because the Japanese fought to the death rather than surrender.

SPMs. The rest were able to move forward against disorganized resistance. The last concentration of defenders was found in a north-shore antitank ditch, which light tanks eliminated by firing 37mm canister rounds and .30-caliber machine guns down the trench line. Namur was declared secured at 1418hrs.

Two Marines view the aftermath of the air and naval pre-landing attacks on Namur. One Japanese report claimed that the weight of air and naval bombardment changed the shape of the island and killed half of the defenders. Despite this, enough Japanese survived to fight and had to be located and neutralized position by position amid the rubble and wreckage. (US Marine Corps)

Engebi Island, Eniwetok Atoll

February 18, 1944

BACKGROUND TO BATTLE

US planning for the seizure of Eniwetok Atoll began in late 1943 under the code name Operation *Catchpole*. Initial planning was based on an attack date of May 1, 1944. By February 2, however, it was evident that the VAC floating reserve would not be needed on Kwajalein Atoll. Rear Admiral Richmond K. Turner then recommended to his superiors that Eniwetok Atoll be attacked as soon as possible using the floating corps' reserve. On February 5, Admiral Nimitz arrived at Kwajalein and met with Vice Admiral Raymond A. Spruance, Turner, and Major General Holland M. Smith about accelerating the date of the Eniwetok operation. Nimitz quickly approved the operation. D-day for Eniwetok Atoll was initially set for February 15, but delayed to February 17 to allow more time to refuel and rearm ships.

Detailed planning and assembling of an attack force had started before Nimitz's approval. On February 3, Rear Admiral Harry W. Hill was ordered to command the attack on Eniwetok Atoll. The attack force (designated TG 51.11) was formed with the floating reserve as the landing force and ships and aircraft from the Roi-Namur and Kwajalein Island attack forces for fire support, escort, and air support. LVTs and LVT(A)s were provided from the US Army force that had assaulted Kwajalein Island. Fire-support ships totaled three battleships, three heavy cruisers, ten destroyers, and six LCI(G)s. Three escort carriers and one task group of fast carriers (one fleet and two light carriers) provided air support. Twelve days after Nimitz's approval, the landings began on Eniwetok Atoll.

The landing force, designated TacGrp 1, was commanded by Brigadier General Thomas E. Watson and included: 22d Marines (with 2d Separate Pack Howitzer Battalion, 2d Separate Tank Company, and support units);

106 RCT (106th Infantry Regiment minus its 2d Battalion but with the 104th Field Artillery Battalion and support units); VAC Reconnaissance Company; Co. D (Scout), 4th Tank Battalion; 708th Provisional Amphibian Tractor Battalion (102 LVTs); Co. A, 708th Amphibian Tank Battalion (17 LVT(A)s); and a provisional US Army amphibious truck (DUKW) company with 30 DUKWs and four LVTs.

As a reserve, the two regiments of TacGrp 1 had not trained to conduct amphibious assaults on atolls. It had been expected that the troops would land across secured beaches. TacGrp 1's intended role was to reinforce assault units and complete the clearing of Japanese resistance. It was a temporary headquarters with an experimental streamlined staff. Its original job was to command the VAC reserve for Operation *Flintlock*, not to conduct a multiregiment amphibious assault. The capture of Eniwetok Atoll proved almost beyond its capacity, according to Colonel Wallace M. Greene: "'I can personally attest,' stated the group G-3, 'that I and all members of the staff came out of the Eniwetok operation utterly exhausted by day and night effort. The streamlined staff idea died a rapid and just death as the staff itself was about to expire'" (quoted in Shaw, Nalty, & Turnbladh 1966: 185).

Eniwetok Atoll was undefended at the start of the Pacific War. The Japanese began building an airstrip on Engebi Island in November 1942 and completed it in mid-1943. In October 1943, a 61-man detachment of the 61st Naval Guard Unit armed with two 120mm guns and infantry weapons arrived from Kwajalein Atoll. After the loss of Tarawa Atoll, the Japanese decided Eniwetok Atoll needed a larger garrison. The 1st Amphibious (or Sea Mobile) Brigade, commanded by Major General Nishida Yoshima, had been assigned to the IJN's Combined Fleet at Truk Atoll in the Carolines as a mobile counterlanding force for the Marshalls. In December, the Japanese decided to use the 1st Amphibious Brigade to reinforce garrisons in the Marshalls. Some combat elements of the brigade went to Kwajalein and the brigade's sea-transportation unit (equipped with motorized coastal barges) was sent to the Palaus. The rest of the brigade, 2,586 men strong, was sent to defend Eniwetok Atoll and arrived on January 4, 1944. Nishida had his brigade headquarters, two battalion headquarters, five rifle companies, two battalion mortar and two battalion artillery companies, two battalion pioneer platoons, the brigade's automatic-cannon company, tank company, engineer unit, and most of its service and medical units. The brigade had about six weeks to prepare defenses.

Before arriving at Eniwetok Atoll, Nishida issued his orders for its defense. Key points in this were:

> 1. Positions must be strong, and must be so planned as to allow for all-around defense.
>
> 2. Try to convert key terrain features into strong points and successively complete permanent installations in vital sectors so that it will be possible to conduct a strong, flexible defense. However, be careful not to jeopardize the safety of the various naval shore installations.
>
> 3. In planning the defenses, pay special attention to the shore line, the ocean bottom, and the depth of water. Erect suitable artificial obstacles along the shore line where landings are anticipated. The importance of splitting up and isolating hostile infantry forces must be remembered.

4. For protection against enemy artillery and bombs, build covered positions, cave-type shelters, and hangars. Use local materials. Prepare at least four alternate positions for heavy weapons, and build individual shelters at least 7 yards apart. In addition, pay attention to dispersion, deployment, and camouflage, so that we will suffer fewer casualties and less damage.

5. Prepare a large number of dummy positions and dummy installations of all kinds. (quoted in MIB III-1: 12–13)

US Navy Douglas SBD-5 Dauntless dive bombers of Composite Squadron 35 (VC-35) fly over the northern part of Eniwetok Atoll, February 18, 1944. The large island below is Engebi. (US Navy/Wikimedia/Public Domain)

Nishida deployed his troops on three of Eniwetok Atoll's islands: Parry, Eniwetok, and Engebi. Nishida's headquarters was established on Parry Island. This island was assigned a 305-man garrison and it was home to the 810-man brigade reserve. In addition, 232 laborers, civilians, and aviation personnel were on the island. Eniwetok Island's defenses were originally manned by 779 men (and 24 civilians) but were reinforced just before the attack by 129 men from the brigade reserve on Parry.

Lieutenant Colonel Yano Toshio (commander of the brigade's 3d Battalion) was assigned to defend Engebi Island. He had his battalion's headquarters company, his 8th Rifle Company (the other two were detached), his battalion's mortar and artillery companies (less one 75mm gun and crew), and its infantry pioneer platoon. Attached were the brigade's 1st Automatic Cannon Platoon, two engineer squads, and the 2d Tank Platoon (three light tanks). A total of 692 men of the 1st Amphibious Brigade were on Engebi along with 44 men of the 61st Naval Guard Unit and 540 assorted naval-aviation ground crew, civilians, and laborers. Engebi's defenders were armed with two 75mm mountain guns, two 20mm automatic cannons, two 120mm naval guns, two 37mm antitank guns, two twin-mount 13mm antiaircraft machine guns, three light tanks, at least 12 light machine guns, two heavy machine guns, 13 grenade dischargers, 12 81mm mortars, one 20mm antitank rifle, and two flamethrowers. Before the US attack, Yano told his men:

> ... if sea and air control are in hostile hands, this garrison must be responsible for its own defense. Because of this, it is essential that we make the utmost use of every available man and of every position that we can possibly fortify. Our plan must be to let the enemy approach the shore line and then annihilate him with withering fire power.
>
> Installations and fortifications on the present defense line must be strengthened, and new tactical positions must be built on the lagoon side of the island. (Quoted in MIB III-1: 120)

On February 13, Yano ordered special attention be given to strengthening those defenses facing the lagoon because US forces had invaded across lagoon beaches at Tarawa Atoll and Kwajalein Atoll. The short time spent fortifying Engebi meant that the Japanese defenses were mainly trenches, dugouts, and coconut-log barricades. Many were provided with whatever top cover could be found. Some strongpoints were built in a spiderweb pattern. At the center of each web was a large personnel shelter built with coconut logs and corrugated iron that had a thick layer of sand over a log roof. Encircling the shelter was a ring of foxholes, about 10–15ft apart, with corrugated-iron roofs and connected by narrow trenches or tunnels. Positions on the perimeter of the web were connected by well-camouflaged radial trenches and tunnels to the shelter, making detection difficult. A few concrete pillboxes with walls 1ft or less thick were built. These pillboxes proved to be not as sturdy as those found on Tarawa Atoll and Kwajalein.

Four centers of resistance were organized on Engebi; the main position was just inland from the center of the lagoon beach, near the southern tip of the island (Skunk Point), near the western tip (Weasel Point), and near the northern tip (Newt Point). The main position was manned by Yano's headquarters, mortar company, automatic-cannon platoon, pioneer platoon, attached engineer squads, and the tank platoon (with its dug-in tanks serving as pillboxes). Skunk Point was held by the 8th Rifle Company (less one platoon) and the 37mm antitank platoon of the artillery company. At Weasel Point were Yano's artillery company (less its 37mm antitank platoon) and the 8th Rifle Company's detached rifle platoon. Newt Point was held by the detachment of the 61st Naval Guard Unit manning the island's two 120mm guns plus miscellaneous IJN personnel.

US aircraft struck the airfield on Engebi on January 30 to neutralize it in preparation for landings on Kwajalein Atoll: 15 IJN medium bombers were destroyed on the ground and several small ships sunk in the lagoon. During February 1–7, and again on February 11 and 13, Eniwetok Atoll was struck by carrier-based aircraft. These attacks destroyed most of the above-ground structures. On February 16, carrier air strikes commenced in preparation for the coming amphibious assault. A Japanese diarist on Engebi wrote of the effect of these air strikes: "When such a small island as Engebi is hit by

A US sailor standing in a Japanese spider hole on Parry Island, Eniwetok Atoll, after its capture. Japanese defenders made extensive use of this type of infantry fighting position. With a camouflaged cover closed over the hole, Marines would not see these spider holes. Defenders would let US troops pass by, then rise up and fire from the rear of the passing Marine. Spider holes were frequently connected by tunnels or covered trenches, allowing Japanese soldiers to move between positions. (US Navy)

about 130 bombs a day, and, having lost its ammunition and provisions, lies helpless, it is no wonder that some soldiers have gone out of their minds" (quoted in Shaw, Nalty, & Turnbladh 1966: 194).

Before dawn on February 17, D-day at Eniwetok Atoll, fire-support ships of TG 51.11 started shelling Engebi, Parry, and Eniwetok islands. An IJA warrant officer on Parry recorded:

> I was amazed at the severity of the bombardment. The bombardment was most severe from 0500 to 0600 ... Everyone was looking on fully prepared for battle ... Planes circled the sky all day, and the bombardment also lasted all day ... There were some who were buried by the shells from the ships ... How many times shall we bury ourselves in the sand. (Quoted in Heinl & Crown 1954: 127)

The eight 16in guns of the battleship USS *Colorado* (BB-45) and the nine 8in guns of the heavy cruiser USS *Louisville* (CA-28) shelled Engebi from the seaward while two groups, each composed of a cruiser and a destroyer, shelled Parry and Eniwetok islands. Once minesweepers had cleared the entrances to the lagoon, other ships of the attack force sailed into it.

At 1119hrs, the battleships USS *Tennessee* (BB-43) and USS *Pennsylvania* (BB-38), each armed with 12 14in guns, opened fire, adding their shells to those of *Colorado* and *Louisville*. While Engebi was being softened up, the VAC Reconnaissance Company landed and secured seven small islets southeast of the island by 1400hrs. Two islets were occupied by TacGrp 1's field artillery, which registered 75mm and 105mm howitzers on the island to support the next day's assault landing by the 22d Marines. Registration was completed at 1902hrs and nighttime harassing fires on the island started at 1930hrs. During the artillery registration, US Navy underwater demolition divers approached to within 50yd of the lagoon beaches while *Tennessee* and *Colorado*, the destroyers USS *Heermann* (DD-532) and USS *McCord* (DD-534), and an LCI(G) fired over their heads. The divers found no mines or obstacles and marked boat lanes and shallow spots with buoys for the assault landing on the next day.

MAP KEY

1 0843hrs: One minute after the cessation of naval shelling lasting one hour and 47 minutes and conducted from positions 1,000yd offshore by the battleships *Colorado*, *Tennessee*, and *Pennsylvania*, heavy cruiser *Louisville*, and four destroyers, the first wave of LVTs carrying BLT 2/22 reaches Engebi's shore in front of the Japanese main defense position. Left to right on Beach Blue 3 are Cos. G, F, and E.

2 0843hrs: The first wave of LVTs carrying BLT 1/22 reaches Beach White 1 to the right of the pier. Left to right are Cos. B, A, and C.

3 c.0850hrs: Cos. E and G start clearing the Japanese main position while Co. F attacks toward Weasel Point.

4 c.0900hrs: Co. A advances toward Newt Point and Co. B clears the area inland of Beach White 1. Co. C attacks toward Skunk Point.

5 1030hrs: The Japanese main defense position is cleared of resistance by Cos. E and G. The Japanese defenders in BLT 2/22's area are reduced to pockets at Weasel Point and Newt Point.

6 c.1000–1100hrs: BLT 3/22, the regimental reserve, lands.

7 1100hrs: Cos. A and B, with tank support, attack into a wooded area between the beaches and the airstrip.

8 1115hrs: Co. C, supported by US Army-manned 105mm self-propelled guns, attacks Skunk Point.

9 c.1300hrs: Co. I, BLT 3/22, is attached to BLT 1/22 and replaces Co. A in the attack toward Newt Point.

10 1456hrs: US forces declare Skunk Point cleared of resistance.

11 1730hrs: BLT 3/22 and the 2d Separate Tank Company reembark on shipping to attack Eniwetok Island the following day.

12 1810hrs: BLT 2/22 eliminates Japanese pockets of resistance at Weasel Point and Newt Point.

13 1830hrs: BLT 1/22 reaches Newt Point after clearing Japanese positions along the north shore.

Battlefield environment

Eniwetok Atoll is near 11°30'N, 162°20'E with a lagoon of approximately 1,900 square miles. Engebi Island is located near the atoll's northern tip. It is roughly triangular, each side being about 1 mile long. The northern side of the island had been cleared and a concrete-surfaced airstrip built. The remainder of the island was covered with mangroves and coconut palms. The island was physically much like any other coral atoll's island: low, rocky, and having poor soil.

Eniwetok Atoll, in common with all the Marshalls, has a hot and humid climate. February's average high temperature is 82.6°F and its average relative humidity is 80.3 percent. These combine to give a heat index of 90°F, making heat prostration and heat exhaustion problems for troops in combat or doing any heavy outside activity. Water supply, as always on atolls, was an issue. Engebi Island's water was brackish and limited; drinking water for the assaulting Marines had to be brought ashore from the amphibious ships.

Engebi, as with other coral atoll islands, was formed through a long, slow, constant, and continual process that began with the disintegration of a barrier reef around a volcanic island. Ocean waves break apart pieces of reef, which erode into tiny grains of sand. The coral debris and sand pile up with drifting seaweed, creating a mass atop part of the reef. Because organic material, including seeds, is present, plants take root. Soon the coral fragments and sand are bound by matted roots of coarse grass and vines. This does not provide ground that is easy for troops to dig positions in.

A road ran along Engebi's southwest side fronting the lagoon beaches. The Japanese had constructed most of their buildings along this road. A pier extended over the reef into the lagoon that was used for loading and unloading small ships. A second road ran inland, crossing the island toward the eastern beach. This road started at a junction located about one-third of the distance along the road from the southernmost point on the island. This second road skirted the beach side of a large palm grove on the east side of the island south of the airfield. This grove provided the only covered terrain on the island.

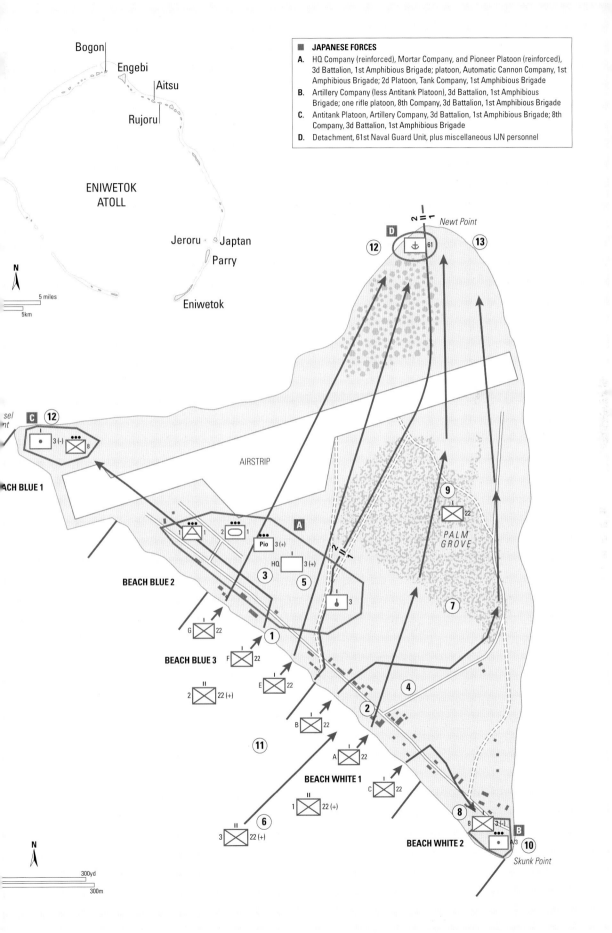

Bogon

Engebi

Aitsu

Rujoru

ENIWETOK
ATOLL

Jeroru · Japtan
Parry

Eniwetok

N

5 miles

5km

JAPANESE FORCES
A. HQ Company (reinforced), Mortar Company, and Pioneer Platoon (reinforced),
3d Battalion, 1st Amphibious Brigade; platoon, Automatic Cannon Company, 1st
Amphibious Brigade; 2d Platoon, Tank Company, 1st Amphibious Brigade
B. Artillery Company (less Antitank Platoon), 3d Battalion, 1st Amphibious
Brigade; one rifle platoon, 8th Company, 3d Battalion, 1st Amphibious Brigade
C. Antitank Platoon, Artillery Company, 3d Battalion, 1st Amphibious Brigade; 8th
Company, 3d Battalion, 1st Amphibious Brigade
D. Detachment, 61st Naval Guard Unit, plus miscellaneous IJN personnel

Newt Point

D

12   61   13

PALM
GROVE

AIRSTRIP

C   12

sel
nt

3 (–)   8

ACH BLUE 1

A

1   1   2   1

Pio   3 (+)

HQ   3 (+)

3   5

3

9   22

7

BEACH BLUE 2

G   22

BEACH BLUE 3

F   22

E   22

2   22 (+)

1

4

B   22

2

11

A   22

BEACH WHITE 1

C   22

1   22 (+)

6   8   8   3 (–)

3   22 (+)   B

BEACH WHITE 2   10

Skunk Point

N

300yd

300m

INTO COMBAT

Engebi Island was attacked by the 22d Marines under Colonel John T. Walker. The landing was executed across the lagoon beaches using two BLTs abreast. A small pier near the middle of the beach separated the BLTs' zones. South of the pier, BLT 1/22 under Lieutenant Colonel Walfried H. Fromhold – followed by 2d Platoon, 2d Separate Tank Company, with M4A2 medium tanks; 1st Platoon, 2d Separate Engineer Company; and two 105mm self-propelled guns of the 106th Infantry Regiment's Cannon Company – landed across Beach White 1. North of the pier, BLT 2/22 under Lieutenant Colonel Donn C. Hart – followed by 2d Separate Tank Company (less 2d Platoon) with M4A2 medium tanks, and 2d Platoon, 2d Separate Engineer Company – assaulted Beach Blue 3. The tanks, engineers, and self-propelled guns were under regimental command. BLT 3/22 was the regimental reserve and the US Army's 106 RCT was held as TacGrp 1's reserve. The two artillery battalions landed the day before were assigned to provide direct support to the 22d Marines.

Each assault BLT was transported in 48 LVTs organized in six waves of eight vehicles each. In each BLT's sector the plan called for an LVT wave to land at Z-hour, one at Z+3 minutes, and one at Z+5. Five LCMs carrying M4A2 medium tanks would land at Z+10, then three more LVT waves would follow at Z+15, Z+17, and Z+20. Following these was a wave of LCMs carrying 75mm and 105mm self-propelled guns which were to land "as soon as possible." The last wave of each BLT was composed of two LCMs carrying bulldozers for the engineers that would land when directed. Each BLT was preceded by six LCI(G)s, three each in echelon on their left and right flanks. Following these were six LVT(A)s arranged similarly. Between the two BLTs was a line of five LVT(A)s.

This aerial photograph shows assault waves of BLT 2/22 (on the left) and BLT 1/22 (on the right) heading for Engebi. The waves are spreading somewhat because of wind, current, and mechanical performance differences. In the center of the formation the apex of LCI(G)s and LVT(A)-1s separating the two BLTs can be seen; the leading LCI(G)s have just fired their 4.5in rocket barrages toward the landing beaches. (US Navy)

An IJA Type 95 Ha-Gō light tank in a dugout position on Engebi Island, Eniwetok Atoll. By the time of the Eniwetok Atoll invasion, IJA senior commanders knew that their light tanks were highly vulnerable to US weapons. Positions like this one may have been intended to provide some protection to tanks from naval shelling and act as pillboxes on the defense. Doctrine called for light tanks to support counterattacks against US troops who reached the beach. On Engebi, no organized counterattacks were made. (US Navy)

At 0655hrs, February 18, *Colorado* and *Louisville* resumed shelling Engebi. *Tennessee* and *Pennsylvania* joined shortly thereafter and fired from stations 1,000yd offshore. Four destroyers added their gunfire to the bombardment. This lasted until approximately 0800hrs when it ceased to allow carrier-based aircraft to strike the island for ten minutes. After five minutes of air bombardment the first wave of LVTs crossed the line of departure. At 0811hrs the ships resumed shelling, which continued until 0842hrs, one minute before the first wave of LVTs transporting BLT 1/22 reached the shore at 0843hrs, two minutes before the planned time. In the minutes before they reached the beach the accompanying LCI(G)s fired 4.5in rocket barrages. Unfortunately, a range-estimation error resulted in the rockets hitting the water. The LCI(G)s kept up fire with their guns while getting as close to the beach as possible. LVT(A)s were with the LVTs and reached the beach at the same time. The assault waves met no opposition as the LVTs crawled over the coral reef and up the beach. Both the LVTs and the LVT(A)s were to advance 100yd inland but were stopped by blown-down palm trees and debris resulting from the preparatory bombardment.

As the Marines debarked from the LVTs, the Japanese began firing. Resistance was disorganized and limited to rifles, light machine guns, grenade dischargers, and a few mortar rounds. Both the intensity of the preparatory bombardment and the short time interval between the ships lifting fire and the Marines landing left the defenders stunned and disoriented. Some Japanese positions near the landing beaches were eliminated with little to no resistance.

BLT 2/22 landed on Beach Blue 3 in front of Yano's main defense position. This position was located within the area of the most intense pre-landing bombardment and contained the Japanese headquarters on Engebi. It is not known what if any actions were taken by Yano during or after the preparatory bombardment. He may have died during the barrage, in combat around his headquarters, or he may have taken his own life. From the beginning of the assault, the island's defenders were reduced to fighting as scattered groups and individuals with no coordination and were unable to organize the intense counterattack called for in their doctrine.

Landing on Engebi Island, February 18, 1944

US view: Engebi Island was assaulted by BLT 1/22 and BLT 2/22 landing abreast on beaches White 1 and Blue 3 using LVT-2s from the US Army's 708th Amphibian Tractor Battalion. The US observer is a rifleman of Co. C, BLT 1/22, riding in an LVT that is approaching Beach White 1. He is looking forward from his position in the rear of the LVT past the crewman manning a .30-caliber Browning M1919 machine gun. In front of him are his fellow Marines of the assault/boat team he is assigned to. His LVT, as are others, is somewhat behind the LVTs in the wave that can be seen from left to right. On the right is Engebi Island's

Skunk Point, a Japanese strongpoint and Co. C's objective. Smoke from the pre-landing air and naval bombardment rises above the island. The Marines in the LVTs are fully equipped with weapons, packs, entrenching tools, etc. Once the LVTs are ashore and stopped, the Marines will debark by climbing over the sides of the vehicle. After debarking, the Marines will soon drop their packs to make it easier to fight. They will carry as much ammunition as possible with them, as well as water, first-aid kits, entrenching tools, and emergency rations (usually candy bars).

Japanese view: The Japanese observer is a message runner of the 8th Rifle Company, 3d Battalion, 1st Amphibious (Sea Mobile) Brigade. He is in the rear of a dugout near Skunk Point at the south-eastern tip of Engebi. He is looking toward the front of the dugout from behind two junior officers and a signalman of his brigade operating a field telephone. His view is through a slit between coconut logs that are part of the dugout's walls. To the right of the officers is an artillery observation telescope. The pre-landing bombardment has ceased as the landing wave closes the final yards to the beach. Before them the officers can see waves

of LVT-2s and LVT(A)-1s approaching the two landing beaches as the LCI(G)s engage targets on the beaches. In the immediate foreground, to the right, is a 37mm Type 94 antitank gun and crew (also from the 1st Amphibious Brigade) in a coconut-log and earth open firing position. The gun chief is leaning on the berm looking toward the LVTs and beach with binoculars. Two ammunition porters have just finished removing camouflage (palm fronds and netting) from around the gun position. In the distance are LVTs in a scattered line. Also visible are LCI(G)s and fire-support ships approximately 1,000yd offshore.

On the 22d Marines' right (White 1), BLT 1/22 attacked with Co. B on the left and Co. A on the right. Co A's 3d Platoon was delayed because several of its LVTs broke down during the ship-to-shore movement. This platoon was to maintain contact with Co. C, which landed minutes behind them and attacked toward Skunk Point. The late arrival of 3d Platoon allowed a gap to develop between Cos. A and C after 0900hrs. When this happened, the platoon stayed with Co. C. Some Japanese around Skunk Point tried to take advantage of this gap to escape from Co. C's attack, but the company plugged it by moving one of its platoons into the gap, sealing off the Skunk Point defenders. Facing several concrete pillboxes, Co. C was reinforced by two US Army-manned 105mm self-propelled guns around 1115hrs. The company continued the slow process of eliminating Japanese defenses around Skunk Point with the 105mm guns using 80 rounds to knock out two pillboxes. At 1456hrs the company declared that Skunk Point was captured.

By 1100hrs, Cos. A and B were attacking into a wooded area between the landing beaches and the airstrip near Newt Point. This area contained dense vegetation including trees, many of which had been knocked down by the preparatory bombardment. Fromhold held his Marines back until they were joined by a platoon of M4A2 medium tanks that had landed at 0900hrs. Dense vegetation, downed trees, and debris slowed the advance, as did numbers of Japanese who had fled to this region from their shore positions and now, trapped, fought fanatically. Like the rest of the island, this area contained trenches and spiderweb defense positions. Finding all the locations within a web was difficult because of the tunnels. Marines quickly solved this problem, once they had found one or more openings: "it was found expedient to toss smoke grenades into these prior to exploding main demolition charges. Thus, the exits were exposed by escaping smoke. These exits were then covered by fire or flame thrower when the main charge was exploded" (Heinl & Crown 1954: 133).

M4A2 medium tanks move across the northern side of Engebi on February 18, 1944. These tanks of the 2d Separate Tank Company were supporting BLT 2/22. The tanks are in the foreground of the photograph, which looks south. This photograph was taken from an aircraft operating from USS *Chenango* (CVE-28), one of the escort carriers providing air support for the attack on Eniwetok Atoll. (US Navy)

A three-man Marine machine-gun crew in position near a Japanese dugout on one of the islands of Eniwetok Atoll. Overhead to the right is a US Navy Douglas SBD Dauntless dive-bomber. Smoke rises in front of the Marines as they watch for enemy movement and snipers. Series F Marine divisions carried 302 .30-caliber light (air-cooled) machine guns, 162 .30-caliber heavy (water-cooled) machine guns, and 161 .50-caliber heavy machine guns. (US Navy)

With one platoon operating with Co. C, Co. A was hard-pressed to cover all its front. Walker therefore attached Co. I (BLT 3/22) to BLT 1/22. Co. I replaced Co. A in the front line and continued the attack through the wooded area while Co. A began to mop up bypassed Japanese defenders. Around 1600hrs, BLT 1/22 reached the northern edge of the wooded area. Co. I reverted to its parent BLT's control and again moved to the front. Moving slowly with tank support, BLT 1/22 cleared the Japanese out of their defenses and by 1830hrs had reached the vicinity of Newt Point and the north shore of the island.

BLT 2/22 on the left had an easier fight despite landing against Yano's main position of resistance. The battalion experienced some confusion when a few LVTs landed up to 200yd to the left, but junior officers and noncommissioned officers promptly moved their men to the correct positions and restored order. Led by Cos. E and F, with Co. G in support, BLT 2/22 quickly overran the defenders and reached the edge of the airfield. Here BLT 2/22 waited for the supporting M4A2 medium tanks while artillery shelled the area to the battalion's front. Once the artillery barrage lifted, Cos. E and G plus tanks moved forward while Co. F started to clear Weasel Point. Three Japanese Type 95 Ha-Gō light tanks were encountered; although dug in as if to be pillboxes, the tanks were quickly knocked out by the heavier US M4A2s. The Marines' rapid advance resulted in Japanese resistance in BLT 2/22's zone being reduced to two pockets by 1030hrs,

Marines and Coast Guard personnel display a Japanese flag captured during the battle for Engebi. Bullet holes are visible in the fabric. (© CORBIS/Corbis via Getty Images)

one at Weasel Point and one at Newt Point. These were both destroyed by 1810hrs.

Although mopping up continued on February 19, the 22d Marines' seizure of Engebi was accomplished in just about ten hours from first landing at 0843hrs to the clearing of resistance near Newt Point around 1830hrs. Even before this, at about 1730hrs the 2d Separate Tank Company and BLT 3/22 had been reembarked on amphibious shipping to participate with the US Army's 106 RCT in the attack on Eniwetok Island the next day.

After Engebi was secured, BLT 3/22 helped the US Army's 106 RCT capture Eniwetok Island on February 19. This photograph shows Marines of BLT 3/22 preparing to advance on Japanese positions on Eniwetok Island and reveals the terrain of the islands of Eniwetok Atoll once Marines and soldiers had landed. Many palm trees still stand after the pre-landing bombardment. These bombardments were directed against specifically identified targets rather than indiscriminate area shelling. (US Navy)

Analysis

LESSONS LEARNED: AMERICAN

In his after-action report on the Tarawa assault, Rear Admiral R.K. Turner, the commander of the 5th Amphibious Force, observed that: "Attack on an atoll resembles in many respects the assault of a fort or fortified locality with, of course, the added complication of having to initiate the assault with the ship to shore movement" (quoted in COMINCH 1944b: 1-4). This reflected what Marines had written in 1933 in the *Tentative Manual for Landing Operations*. In subsequent observations Turner reiterated other subjects, now backed by combat experiences at Tarawa, that Marines identified in their 1933 draft landing manual. Despite problems and heavy casualties, the Tarawa attack validated the fundamental US doctrine for opposed amphibious assaults. Immediately after Tarawa the Navy and Marines (along with the Army) set to work to identify lessons learned and develop new equipment, technologies, tactics, techniques, and procedures to remedy any shortcomings, enhance force capabilities, and reduce future casualties. Included were changes and refinements to ship-to-shore maneuver, naval-gunfire support, command and communications, and intelligence.

With regard to ship-to-shore maneuver, using LVTs as assault troop carriers was an innovation at Tarawa Atoll. These provided a means to deliver troops to the beach across coral reefs. The attack on Tarawa Atoll demonstrated that one LVT battalion per division was not enough; it was recognized that each assault regiment required an LVT battalion to lift it. Therefore the LVT force was expanded such that on Roi-Namur, two battalions plus one company were used by the 4th Marine Division alone. Additionally, the overland movement capability of LVTs could get troops inland before debarking. Taking advantage of this, LVT boat teams fought as provisional fighting formations on Roi-Namur. This allowed assault troops to maintain momentum and overrun beach defenses before pausing to reorganize into their normal platoons. LVT(A)s armed with 37mm guns were added after

the fight for Tarawa Atoll and provided additional fire support to assaulting troops on beaches and immediately inland. Although not tanks, the LVT(A)s could provide ad hoc "armor" support to infantry until their supporting light and medium tanks were landed.

In terms of naval-gunfire support, before Tarawa Atoll many US Navy officers believed that Japanese defenders would be destroyed by the massive naval gunfire available for use. At least one veteran US Navy officer – Rear Admiral Herbert B. Knowles – disagreed and recalled stating his concerns before the operation: "... very forcibly during a conference at Wellington, N.Z. I had witnessed a similar bombing and bombardment of Gavutu Island, in the Solomons, where I landed a Marine Paratroop outfit. From daylight to noon this little island was subjected to repeated bombing attacks and bombardment by cruisers and destroyers. The results had been most disappointing" (quoted in Shaw, Nalty, & Turnbladh 1966: 36). The attack on Tarawa Atoll verified this skepticism. In response, the US Navy built replicas of some of Tarawa Atoll's defensive structures on gunnery ranges in Hawaii to test ammunition, shelling techniques, and their effects. These also served as training targets for fire-support ships.

Another fire-support issue at Tarawa Atoll was that cessation of the bombardment 20 minutes before the lead wave of LVTs hit the beach gave the defenders time to recover from the effects of the barrage and man their firing positions. After reviewing the performance of naval gunfire, US Navy leadership decided that ships must get as close as possible to the shore during preparation bombardments and while firing in support of troops during the ship-to-shore assault. Now destroyers closed the beach and relied on observing the progress toward the beach of assault waves before lifting their fires off the beach. Battleships were expected to get within 1,000yd or less of the beach to deliver pinpoint shelling instead of cruising miles offshore and blindly shelling geographical areas. Captains of fire-support ships entered a new age regarding risking their ships. Before the invasion of the Marshalls, Turner decreed: "I say to you commanders of ships – your mission is to put the troops ashore and support their attack to the limit of your capabilities. We expect to lose some ships! If your mission demands it, risk your ship!" (quoted in Shaw, Nalty, & Turnbladh 1966: 124).

To help provide fire support during the final minutes before landing troops hit the beach, LCI(G)s armed with guns and rockets were added to the attack force. These vessels, approaching as close as possible to the coral reefs, provided 4.5in rocket barrages and gunfire to suppress the enemy just as the landing force reached the beach.

With respect to command and communications, during the Tarawa Atoll assault, USS *Maryland* served as the command ship for US Navy and US Marine Corps senior leaders. The battleship had been fitted with a large number of extra radios needed for communications with all the subordinate (sea, air, and land) units and was overcrowded with the Navy and Marine commanders' staffs. Additionally, *Maryland* was one of the fire-support ships and had to stay in its fire-support station. When the 16in guns of its main battery fired, the extra radios frequently failed, rendering the senior commanders out of touch with subordinates at critical moments. Being tied to a fire-support station, the commanders and staffs were unable to move around the attack force to observe and influence critical actions. The solution came in the form of the new amphibious command ship, designated AGC (Auxiliary General Command). These provided large and reliable communications suites, plenty of staff space, more accommodations, and a ship that was dedicated to command and control independent of other duties.

Intelligence officers and planners had to rely heavily on aerial photography. Every opportunity was now taken to include photoreconnaissance flights with air strikes on possible island targets by both the fast carrier task force and land-based aircraft. Photos were taken from all possible angles to provide views for photo interpreters to study, to identify defensive positions, troop accommodations (to estimate garrison sizes), artillery batteries, command posts, reserve dispositions, lines of communications, and more. Intelligence translators became highly valued personnel. They translated captured documents, diaries, communications records, etc., to piece together enemy plans, movements, and orders of battle. Translated documents captured on Kwajalein Atoll revealed the weak state of defenses on Eniwetok Atoll and identified the IJA's 1st Amphibious Brigade as the atoll's garrison, and were critical to the decision to accelerate the seizure of Eniwetok Atoll.

Absorbing the lessons learned at Tarawa Atoll contributed to success during the Marshalls operation. Commanders still noted room for more improvement, especially for future attacks against tougher defenses. In his after-action report on the Marshalls' operation, Major General Smith, CG VAC, commented: "In the attack of coral atolls very few recommendations can be made to improve upon the basic techniques previously recommended and utilized in FLINTLOCK. However, there is still much to be desired to improve planning, improve coordination of efforts and prepare for the attack of more difficult objectives" (quoted in Shaw, Nalty, & Turnbladh 1966: 227). Smith was already thinking ahead to invasions of the larger volcanic islands of Micronesia.

Successful amphibious assaults in the Gilberts and Marshalls were made possible by both the Fast Carrier Task Force and the Pacific Fleet Submarine Force. Fast carriers destroyed Japanese air power before the amphibious force reached the objectives, assisted in bombing and shelling defenses, cut supply lines, and neutralized the IJN's Combined Fleet. Submarines sank Japanese troop and cargo ships on their way to the islands, thereby denying the islands' reinforcements, equipment, and much-needed construction supplies. One important sinking was that of *Bangkok Maru*, transporting the IJA's 800-man

1st South Seas Detachment, which kept this reinforcement from reaching Tarawa Atoll.

LESSONS LEARNED: JAPANESE

Japanese garrisons in the Gilberts and Marshalls were originally components of an intended air–sea–ground battle against an attacking US Pacific Fleet. This plan was discarded in early November 1943 in the face of the heavy losses of Japanese carrier aircrew in the northern Solomons and severe damage to most of the IJN's heavy cruisers by US air strikes at Rabaul. Now weakened, the Combined Fleet could not risk battle with the US Navy's Fifth Fleet. The Gilberts and Marshalls became expendable outposts. Their defenders were ordered to fight as long as possible in order to give Japanese submarines and land-based aviation opportunities to sink US Navy ships. Large-scale land-based air attacks were not launched, however, and few submarines were sent.

Japanese defense doctrine also called for reinforcing islands under attack and conducting counterlandings. The Japanese initially responded to the attack on Tarawa Atoll by organizing a seaborne counterlanding force of one reinforced infantry battalion and sent it to Kwajalein Atoll. Once there, the counterattack was canceled and the troops reinforced local garrisons. How the IJN expected this small force to reach, let alone retake, Tarawa Atoll is not known. This overly optimistic plan ignored the size of the US forces, a trait evident in many Japanese plans during the Pacific War.

What little information the Japanese could glean from fighting on atolls appeared to reinforce their doctrine; to them the attack on Tarawa Atoll proved it was critical to defeat a landing on the shore and, should an invader establish a beachhead, savage counterattacks had to be launched in order to throw the invader back into the sea. In the end, however, no matter how hard an isolated atoll's defenders fought, without the Combined Fleet defeating the US Pacific Fleet and delivering reinforcements, the defenders were doomed to defeat. For Japanese sailors and soldiers on invaded Central Pacific atolls, this meant death in combat, or suicide.

Japanese POWs captured during the Tarawa Atoll operation, November 1943. (US Navy/Wikimedia/Public Domain)

Aftermath

LVTs head for shore as part of the first landing wave on Saipan in the Marianas, June 15, 1944. Having digested the lessons learned from previous landings, the 5th Amphibious Force and VAC executed their largest assault to date; the 2d and 4th Marine divisions each landed four BLTs abreast on an eight-battalion front. In 20 minutes, 700 LVTs and 8,000 Marines were ashore. (US Navy)

On February 25, 1944, the last pockets of Japanese resistance were eliminated on Eniwetok Atoll and US forces were within 1,100 miles of the Marianas. The Central Pacific front was pushed some 800 miles west. Japan's defense line now stretched from the Kurile Islands through the Bonins, Marianas, and Carolines, culminating in New Guinea. The Central Pacific amphibious forces' next attack would not occur until June 1944. Until then, the US Navy's fast carriers would rampage across the ocean, neutralizing the IJN's base at Truk Atoll in the Carolines, whittling down Japanese naval and air power, and supporting General Douglas MacArthur's long-range amphibious attack at Hollandia in New Guinea in April 1944.

After the fight for Tarawa Atoll, the 2d Marine Division went to Hawaii to rest, refit, reorganize, absorb replacements, and train for its next operation. Shortly after Roi-Namur was secured, the 4th Marine Division went to Maui and prepared for its next assault mission. Both divisions next went into action on June 15, 1944, when they assaulted Japanese-held Saipan in the Marianas. After capturing Saipan, the 2d and 4th Marine divisions then attacked Tinian

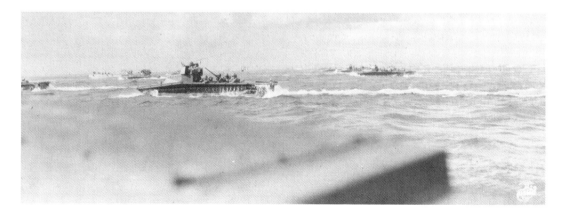

Island, also in the Marianas, on July 24, 1944, staging from Saipan. The 22d Marines moved to Guadalcanal in the Solomons, where the regiment was paired with the 4th Marines in the 1st Provisional Marine Brigade. There the brigade prepared for its next job, the recapture of Guam, the southernmost of the Marianas, along with the 3d Marine Division. Later, the 1st Provisional Marine Brigade was enlarged to become the 6th Marine Division and fought on Okinawa, the southernmost and smallest of the five main islands of Japan.

Capturing Tarawa, Kwajalein, Eniwetok, and other undefended or lightly defended atolls, isolated the remaining Japanese-held atolls in the Marshalls: Wotje, Maloelap, Mille, and Jaluit. From November 1943 until the end of the Pacific War, these four atolls, which the Japanese had planned to use as "unsinkable aircraft carriers," were subjected to land-based air attacks and naval shelling during which almost 13,000 tons of bombs were dropped. Without aircraft, these bases had no offensive capability. The only means of resupply was an occasional visit by an IJN submarine. Life on these isolated atolls was not pleasant. Garrison troops had to farm and fish for food and starvation and disease took a toll. On December 23, 1943, there were 5,101 Japanese holding Mille Atoll. When Japan surrendered, only 2,511 remained alive. After the Pacific War, the IJN second-in-command of Mille Atoll answered the following American questions:

> Q. How did you keep your men busy after the 1st of January 1944? A. The main occupation was making gardens to provide food. Q. Did you build up your protection more? Was that important? A. We were very assiduous in building fortifications until June 1944 then we gave up the idea. We felt it was more worthwhile to grow food than to build fortifications. Q. How many do you estimate died from other causes than bomb wounds? A. Another 1200 deaths resulted from other causes such as lack of food, eating poisonous fish, diseases such as beri-beri, dysentery. Nobody escaped. (USSBS Interrogation No. 93 1945)

The conflict in the Central Pacific was a naval war; without a fleet to oppose the US Navy, Japanese-held atolls and islands became death traps. Either their garrisons were destroyed by amphibious assaults or they were left behind to wither away as the US forces' advance continued westward.

Bypassed atolls in the Marshalls were subjected to systematic air attack during the remainder of World War II. The 4th Marine Air Wing was tasked with keeping the atolls suppressed. These images show the effect of six months of air bombardment of Emidj Island on Jaluit Atoll. By the end of the Pacific War, isolated Japanese garrisons concentrated their efforts toward obtaining food. (US Air Force)

UNIT ORGANIZATIONS

US Marine Corps

The Series E infantry battalion had a battalion headquarters and headquarters company (137 officers and men), three rifle companies (196 officers and men each), and a weapons company (288 officers and men).

Each rifle company consisted of a 28-man headquarters, one 37-man weapons platoon, and three 43-man rifle platoons. Weapons platoons manned three 60mm M2 mortars and three M1919A4 light machine guns. Rifle platoons had a six-man command team and three 12-man rifle squads. Each squad was armed with two Browning Automatic Rifles, two M1 carbines, one M1903 Springfield rifle with grenade launcher, and seven M1 Garand rifles.

The weapons company had a 41-man headquarters, three 43-man machine-gun platoons, and a 58-man mortar platoon. A machine-gun platoon had two sections manning two heavy machine guns each for a total of 12 per company. The mortar platoon had four 81mm mortars.

Companies were designated by letters within the regiment. The 1st Battalion had rifle companies A, B, and C; its weapons company was D. The 2d Battalion's rifle companies were E, F, and G, with H as its weapons company. The 3d Battalion had I, K, and L as its rifle companies and M as its weapons company.

The Series E infantry regiment also had a regimental weapons company of 197 officers and men. This company had a 69-man headquarters, three 34-man antitank platoons each with four 37mm antitank guns, and one 26-man platoon with two halftrack-mounted 75mm guns designated as M3 SPMs.

Japanese forces

The nominal SNLF formation was based on a 1939 Table of Organization structure of three rifle companies, one artillery company, a headquarters, and support units. Personnel totaled 42 officers and 1,158 other ranks. The rifle company had: a 34-man headquarters platoon; three rifle platoons, each with a three-man headquarters, three 11-man rifle squads with nine rifles and a light machine gun, and one 11-man grenadier squad with four grenade dischargers; and a machine-gun platoon with a three-man headquarters, four eight-man machine-gun squads each with one medium machine gun, and two 11-man ammunition squads. The artillery company had a 38-man headquarters platoon, two 36-man infantry-gun platoons (each with two 70mm infantry guns), and two 51-man mountain-gun platoons (each with two 75mm guns).

The battalions of the IJA amphibious brigade each had three rifle companies, a mortar company, a battalion artillery company, and an infantry pioneer platoon. Each of the rifle companies had (on paper) 197 men equipped with 118 Type 99 rifles, 12 grenade dischargers, 12 light machine guns, two heavy machine guns, two 81mm mortars, and one 20mm antitank rifle. The mortar company was authorized 141 men and 12 81mm mortars. The 121-man battalion artillery company had three 75mm regimental guns and two 37mm antitank guns. The 66-man infantry pioneer platoon was an assault unit and was armed with 63 Type 99 rifles, two flamethrowers, three 81mm mortars, and one 50mm mortar. These battalions did not use the 70mm infantry gun as did most IJA battalions.

BIBLIOGRAPHY

Primary sources

CinCPac-CinCPOA (1945). *Japanese Naval Ground Forces*. "Know Your Enemy," CinCPac-CinCPOA Bulletin 11-45. Available at https://www.ibiblio.org/hyperwar/USN/ref/KYE/CINCPAC-11-45/index.html

COMINCH (1944a). *Amphibious Operations During the Period August to December 1943*. United States Fleet, Headquarters Commander in Chief, April 1944 (declassified).

COMINCH (1944b). *Amphibious Operations, the Marshall Islands, January–February 1944.* United States Fleet, Headquarters Commander in Chief, May 1944 (declassified).

Ellis, Major E.H. (1921). *Advanced Base Operations in Micronesia.* Reprinted as FMFRP 12-46, US Marine Corps 1992. Available at www.ibiblio.org/hyperwar/USMC/ref/AdvBaseOps/index.html

FMFRP 12-90 (1991). *Second Marine Division Report on Gilbert Islands Tarawa Operation.* Available at https://www.ibiblio.org/hyperwar/USMC/rep/Tarawa/2dMarDiv-AR.html#BnRpts

FTP-167 (1938). *Landing Operations Doctrine: United States Navy.* Office of the Chief of Naval Operation, Division of Training. Available at https://archive.org/details/landingoperation00unit_0

Heinl, Lieutenant Colonel R.D. & Lieutenant Colonel J.A. Crown (1954). *The Marshalls: Increasing the Tempo.* Historical Branch, G-3 Division Headquarters, US Marine Corps.

MIB III-1 (1944). *Military Intelligence Bulletin Vol. III, No. 1.* Military Intelligence Service, War Department, Washington, DC, September 1944 (declassified). Available at https://cgsc.contentdm.oclc.org/digital/collection/p4013coll8/id/2060

MISLS (1945). "Information Pertaining to Island Warfare Against the United States." Translation of *Taibei Toshosen No Sanko* (March 1944). Fort Snelling, MN: Military Intelligence Service Language School.

Second Demobilization Bureau (1951). *Inner South Seas Islands Area Naval Operations, Part II: Marshall Islands Operations.* Japanese Monograph 173. Military History Section, Japanese Research Division, Headquarters, Army Forces Far East.

Second Demobilization Bureau (1952). *Inner South Seas Islands Area Naval Operations, Part I: Gilbert Islands Operations.* Japanese Monograph 161. Military History Section, Japanese Research Division, Headquarters, Army Forces Far East.

Shaw, H.I., Jr., B.C. Nalty, & E.T. Turnbladh (1966). *Central Pacific Drive: History of U. S. Marine Corps Operations in World War II, Vol. III.* Historical Branch, G-3 Division, Headquarters, US Marine Corps.

Stockman, Captain J.R. (1947). *The Battle for Tarawa.* Historical Branch, G-3 Division, Headquarters, US Marine Corps.

Tentative Manual for Landing Operations (1933). Headquarters, US Marine Corps, Washington, DC. Available at https://cgsc.contentdm.oclc.org/digital/collection/p4013coll11/id/2281

TM-E-30-480 (1944). *Handbook on Japanese Military Forces.* War Department Technical Manual TME-30-480, October 1, 1944. Available at https://www.ibiblio.org/hyperwar/Japan/IJA/HB/

USSBS Interrogation No. 93 (1945). *United States Strategic Bombing Survey Pacific, Interrogations of Japanese Officials.* Interrogation Naval No. 18, USSBS No. 93, October 1945. Available at https://www.ibiblio.org/hyperwar/AAF/USSBS/IJO/IJO-18.html

Secondary sources

Adachi, Austin (2020). *Rikusentai: The Illustrated Encyclopedia of Japanese Naval Landing Forces 1927–1945.* Monee, IL: Rikusentai Publishing.

Adams, Gregg (2021). *Japanese Soldier vs US Soldier: New Guinea 1942–44.* Combat 60. Oxford: Osprey Publishing.

Alexander, Colonel J.H., Ret. (1995) *Utmost Savagery: The Three Days of Tarawa.* Annapolis, MD: Naval Institute Press.

Diamond, Jon (2015). *Chindit vs Japanese Infantryman: 1943–44.* Combat 10. Oxford: Osprey Publishing.

Gilbert, O.E., & R. Caniere (2015). *Tanks in Hell: A Marine Corps Tank Company on Tarawa.* Oxford: Casemate.

Morison, S.E. (1984). *Aleutians, Gilberts and Marshalls, June 1942–April 1944.* History of United States Naval Operations in World War II, Vol. 7. New York, NY: Little, Brown & Co.

Rottman, G.L. (2004a). *US Marine Corps Pacific Theater of Operations 1943–44.* Battle Orders 7. Oxford: Osprey Publishing.

Rottman, G.L. (2004b). *The Marshall Islands 1944: Operation Flintlock: The capture of Kwajalein and Eniwetok.* Campaign 146. Oxford: Osprey Publishing.

Rottman, G.L. (2014). *US Marine vs Japanese Infantryman: Guadalcanal 1942–43.* Combat 8. Oxford: Osprey Publishing.

Wright, Derrick (2000). *Tarawa 1943: The turning of the tide.* Campaign 77. Oxford: Osprey Publishing.

INDEX